Garfield makes it big

BY JIM DAVIS

Ballantine Books • **New York**

2005 Ballantine Books Trade Paperback Edition

Copyright © 1985, 2005 by PAWS, Inc. All Rights Reserved.

Published in the United States by Ballantine Books, an imprint of The Random House Publishing Group,
a division of Random House, Inc., New York.

Ballantine and colophon are registered trademarks of Random House, Inc.

"GARFIELD" and the GARFIELD characters are trademarks of PAWS, Inc.

Originally published in slightly different form in the United States by Ballantine Books, an imprint of
The Random House Publishing Group, a division of Random House, Inc., in 1985.

Library of Congress Control Number: 2005903206

ISBN 0-345-46468-0

Printed in the United States of America

Ballantine Books website address: www.ballantinebooks.com

9 8 7 6 5 4 3 2 1

First colorized editon

Garfield's Loves & Hates

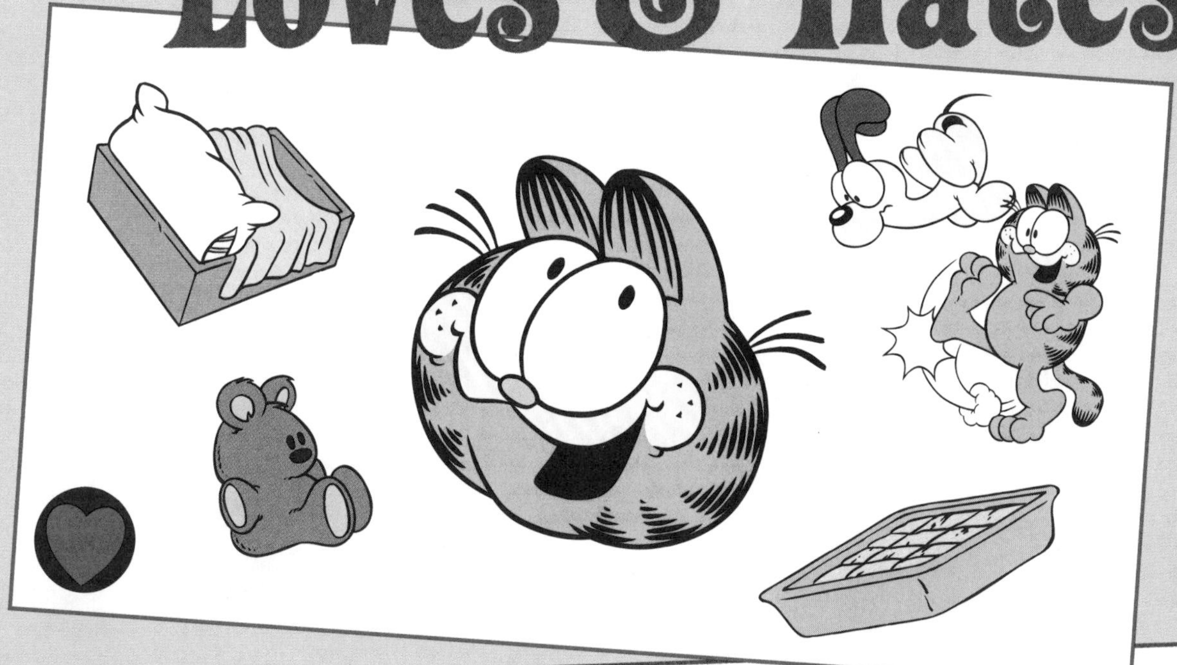

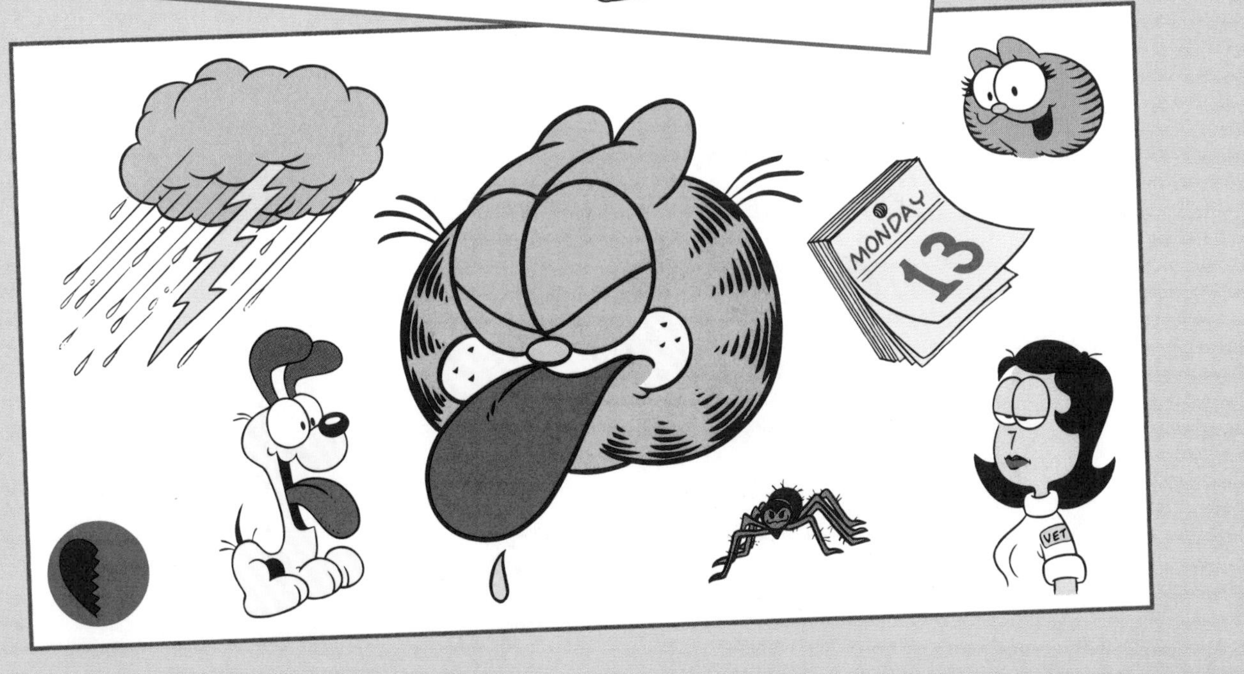
MONDAY
13
VET

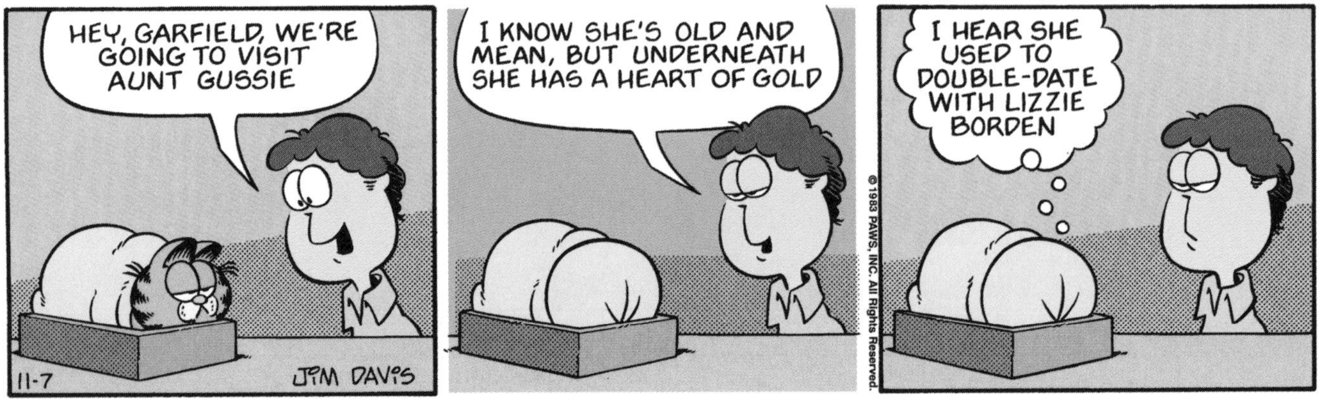
HEY, GARFIELD, WE'RE GOING TO VISIT AUNT GUSSIE
11-7
JIM DAVIS
I KNOW SHE'S OLD AND MEAN, BUT UNDERNEATH SHE HAS A HEART OF GOLD
© 1983 PAWS, INC. All Rights Reserved.
I HEAR SHE USED TO DOUBLE-DATE WITH LIZZIE BORDEN

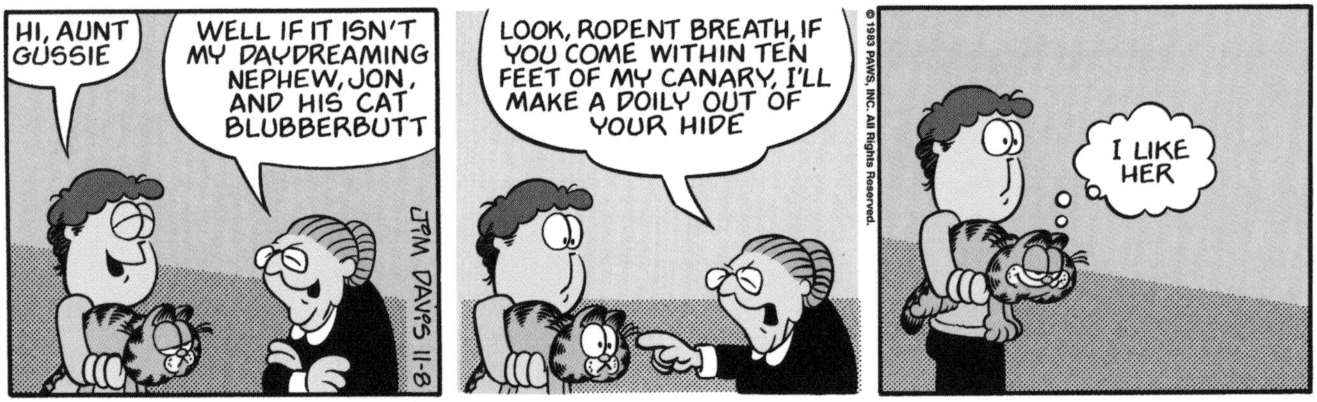
HI, AUNT GUSSIE
WELL IF IT ISN'T MY DAYDREAMING NEPHEW, JON, AND HIS CAT BLUBBERBUTT
JIM DAVIS 11-8
LOOK, RODENT BREATH, IF YOU COME WITHIN TEN FEET OF MY CANARY, I'LL MAKE A DOILY OUT OF YOUR HIDE
© 1983 PAWS, INC. All Rights Reserved.
I LIKE HER

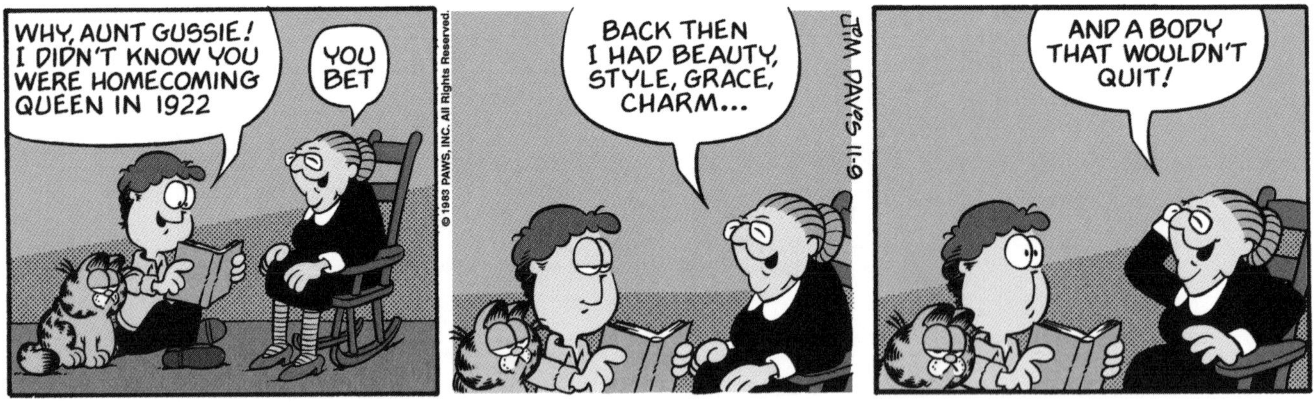
WHY, AUNT GUSSIE! I DIDN'T KNOW YOU WERE HOMECOMING QUEEN IN 1922
YOU BET
© 1983 PAWS, INC. All Rights Reserved.
BACK THEN I HAD BEAUTY, STYLE, GRACE, CHARM...
JIM DAVIS 11-9
AND A BODY THAT WOULDN'T QUIT!

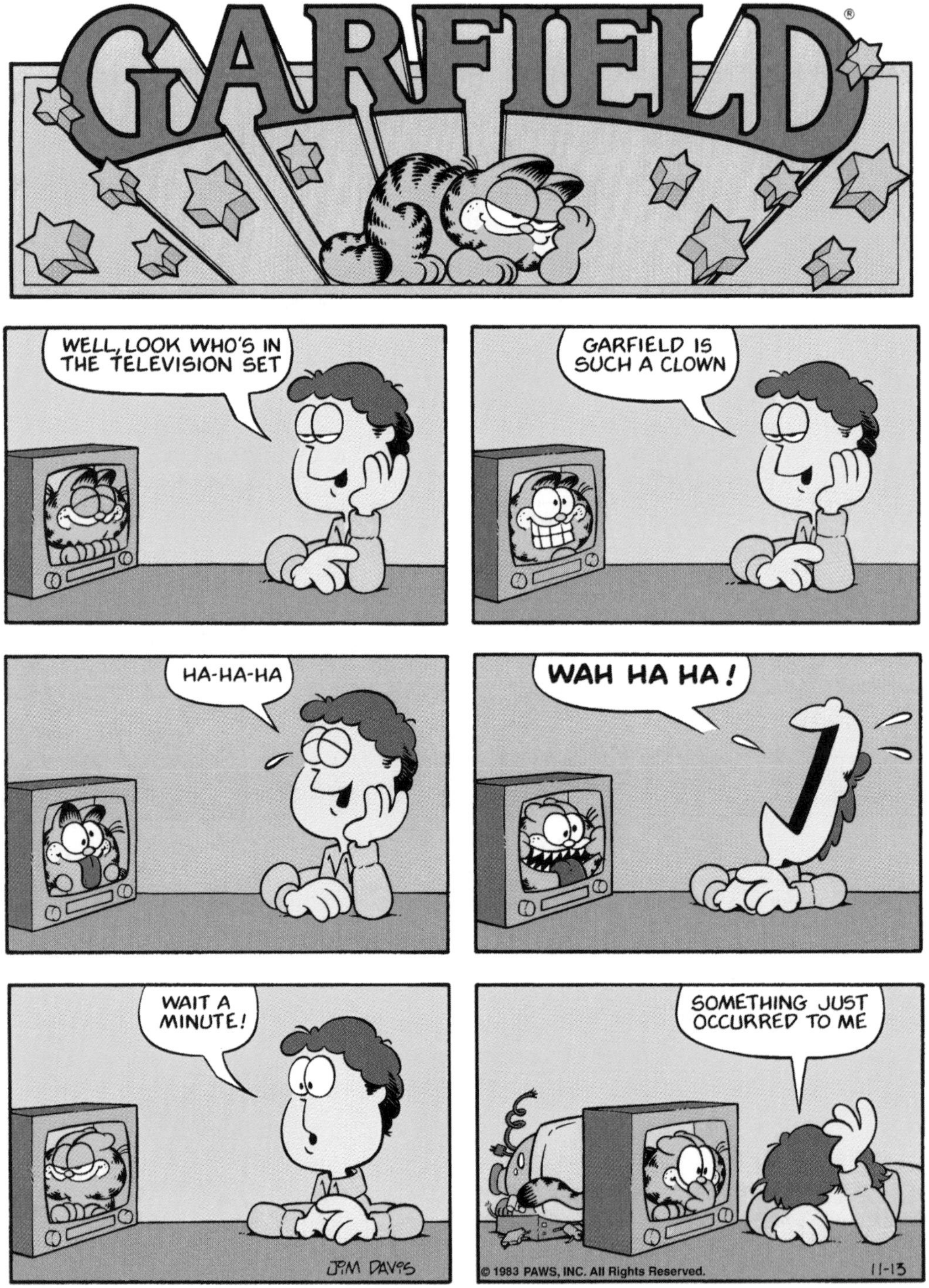
GARFIELD®
WELL, LOOK WHO'S IN THE TELEVISION SET
GARFIELD IS SUCH A CLOWN
HA-HA-HA
WAH HA HA!
WAIT A MINUTE!
SOMETHING JUST OCCURRED TO ME
JIM DAVIS
© 1983 PAWS, INC. All Rights Reserved.
11-13

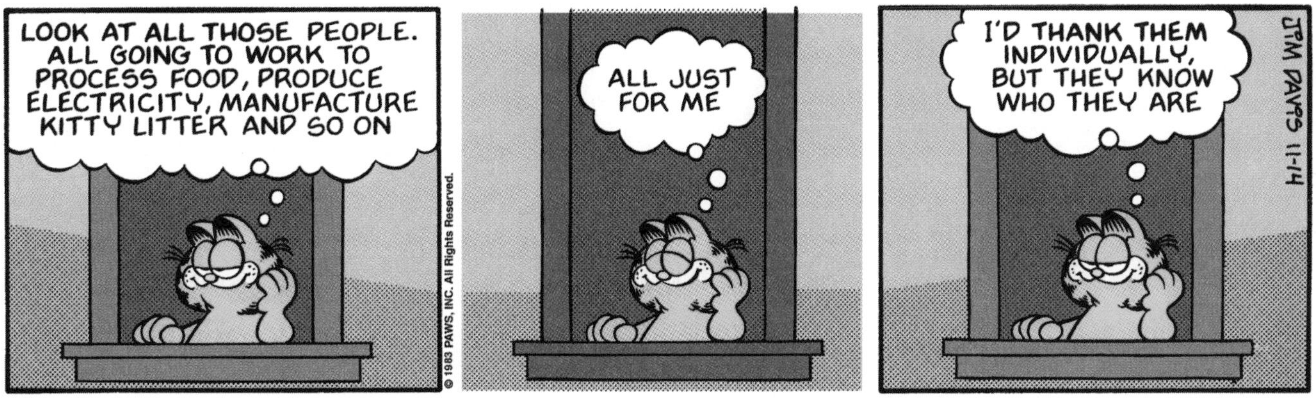
LOOK AT ALL THOSE PEOPLE. ALL GOING TO WORK TO PROCESS FOOD, PRODUCE ELECTRICITY, MANUFACTURE KITTY LITTER AND SO ON
© 1983 PAWS, INC. All Rights Reserved.
ALL JUST FOR ME
I'D THANK THEM INDIVIDUALLY, BUT THEY KNOW WHO THEY ARE
JIM DAVIS 11-14

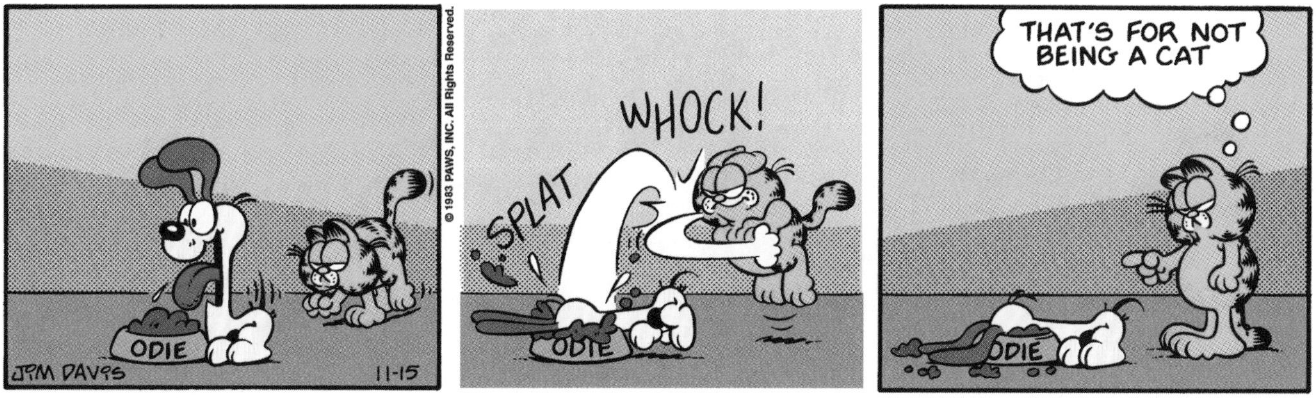
ODIE
JIM DAVIS
11-15
© 1983 PAWS, INC. All Rights Reserved.
WHOCK!
SPLAT
ODIE
THAT'S FOR NOT BEING A CAT
ODIE

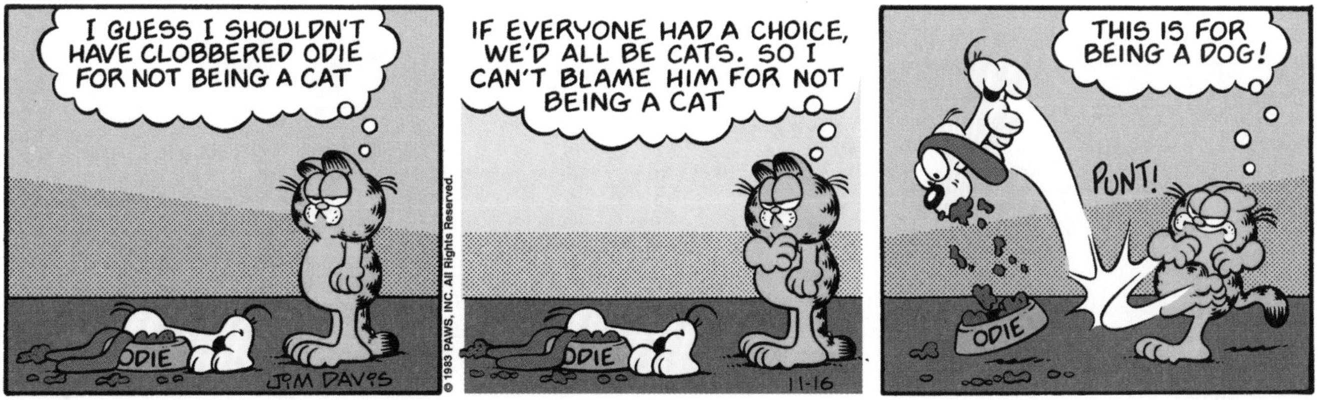
I GUESS I SHOULDN'T HAVE CLOBBERED ODIE FOR NOT BEING A CAT
ODIE
JIM DAVIS
© 1983 PAWS, INC. All Rights Reserved.
IF EVERYONE HAD A CHOICE, WE'D ALL BE CATS. SO I CAN'T BLAME HIM FOR NOT BEING A CAT
ODIE
11-16
THIS IS FOR BEING A DOG!
PUNT!
ODIE

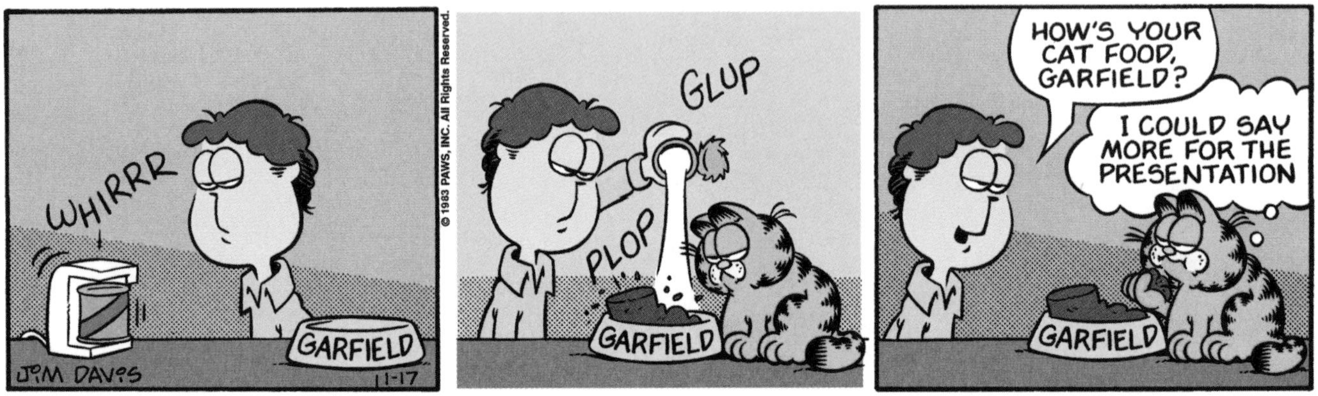
WHIRRR
JIM DAVIS
11-17
GARFIELD
© 1983 PAWS, INC. All Rights Reserved.
GLUP
PLOP
GARFIELD
HOW'S YOUR CAT FOOD, GARFIELD?
I COULD SAY MORE FOR THE PRESENTATION
GARFIELD

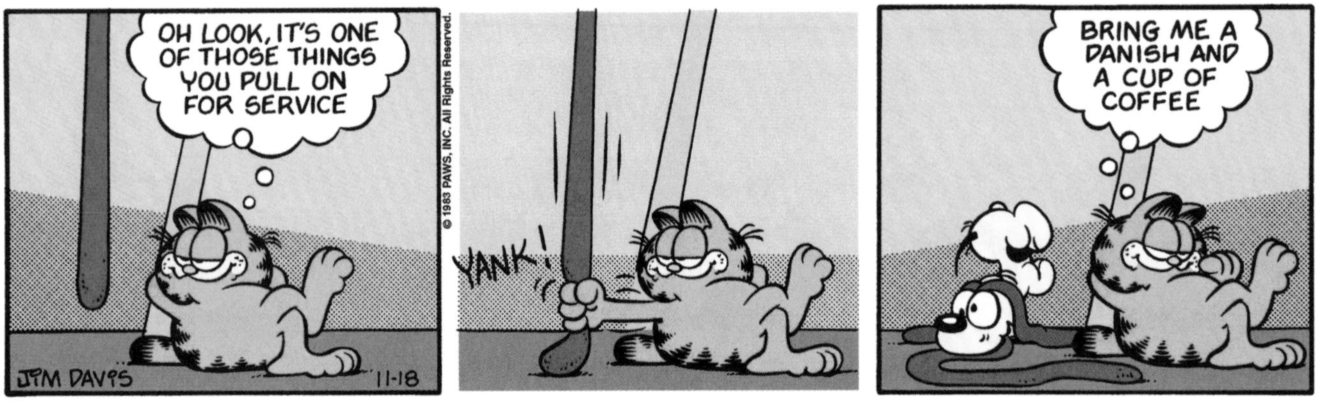
OH LOOK, IT'S ONE OF THOSE THINGS YOU PULL ON FOR SERVICE
JIM DAVIS
11-18
© 1983 PAWS, INC. All Rights Reserved.
YANK!
BRING ME A DANISH AND A CUP OF COFFEE

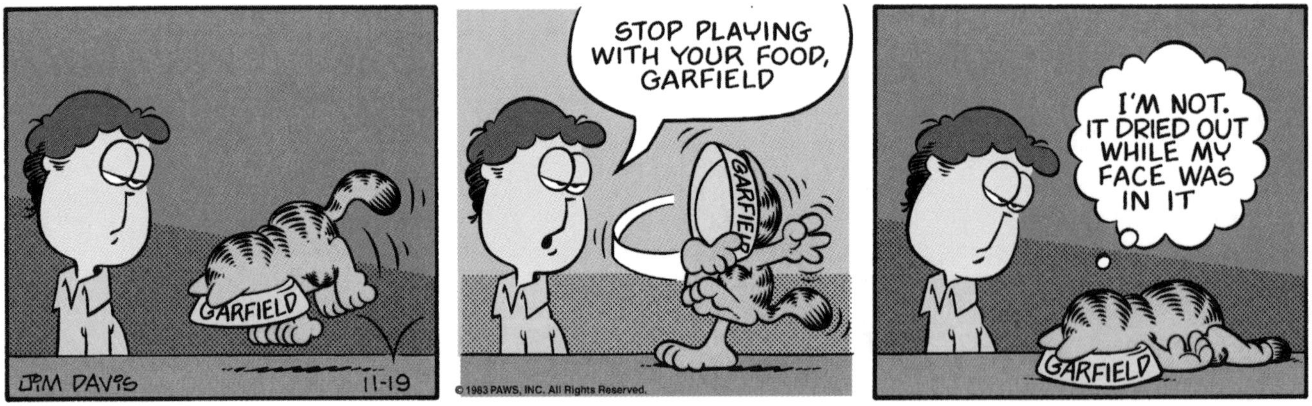
GARFIELD
JIM DAVIS
11-19
STOP PLAYING WITH YOUR FOOD, GARFIELD
GARFIELD
© 1983 PAWS, INC. All Rights Reserved.
I'M NOT. IT DRIED OUT WHILE MY FACE WAS IN IT
GARFIELD

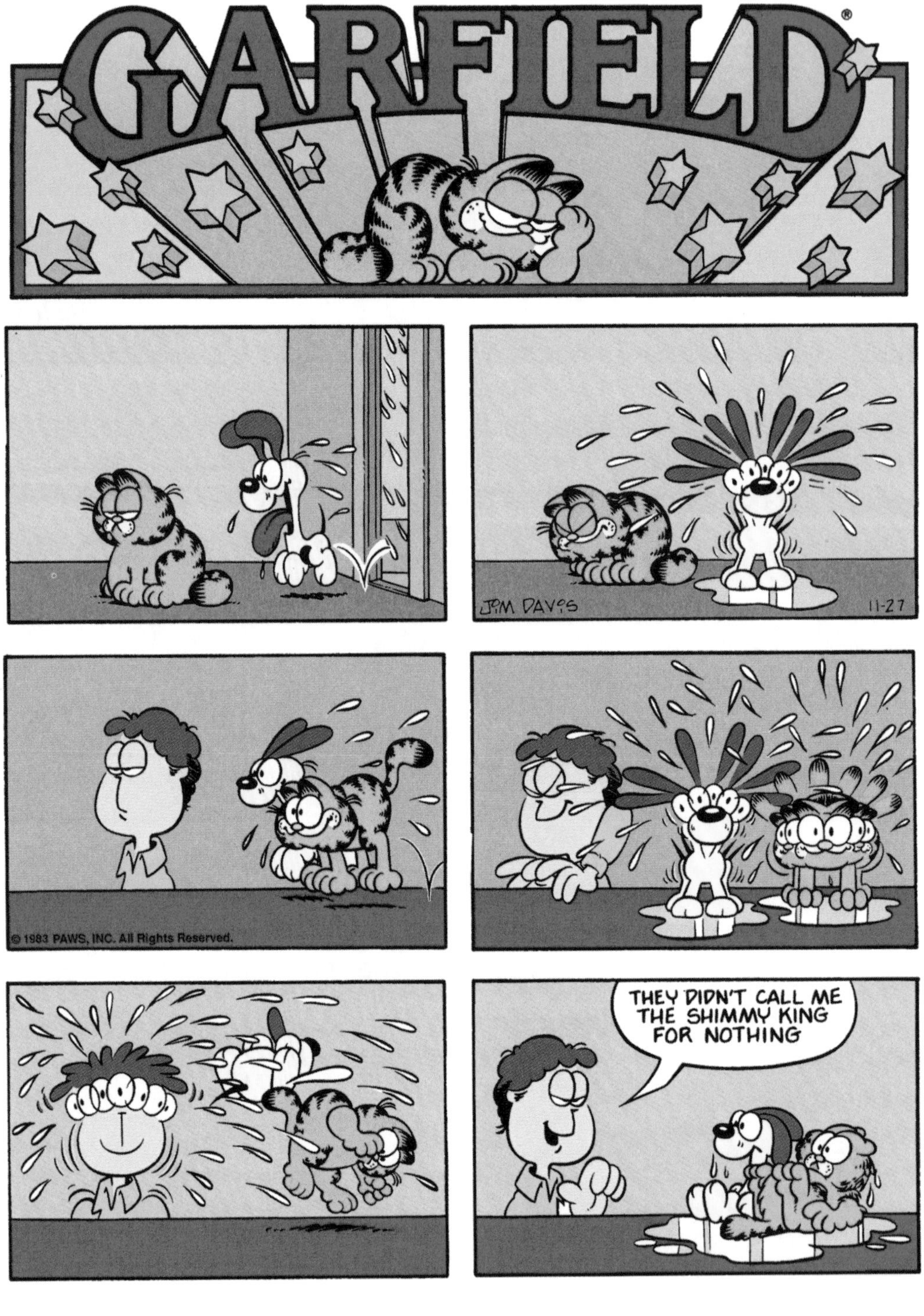
GARFIELD
JIM DAVIS
11-27
© 1983 PAWS, INC. All Rights Reserved.
THEY DIDN'T CALL ME THE SHIMMY KING FOR NOTHING

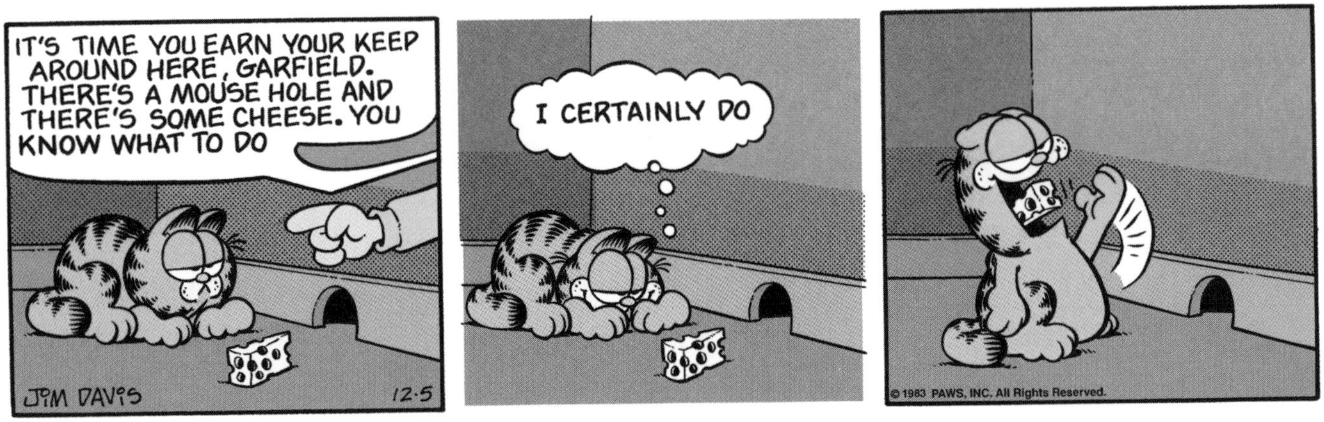
IT'S TIME YOU EARN YOUR KEEP AROUND HERE, GARFIELD. THERE'S A MOUSE HOLE AND THERE'S SOME CHEESE. YOU KNOW WHAT TO DO
I CERTAINLY DO
JIM DAVIS 12·5
© 1983 PAWS, INC. All Rights Reserved.

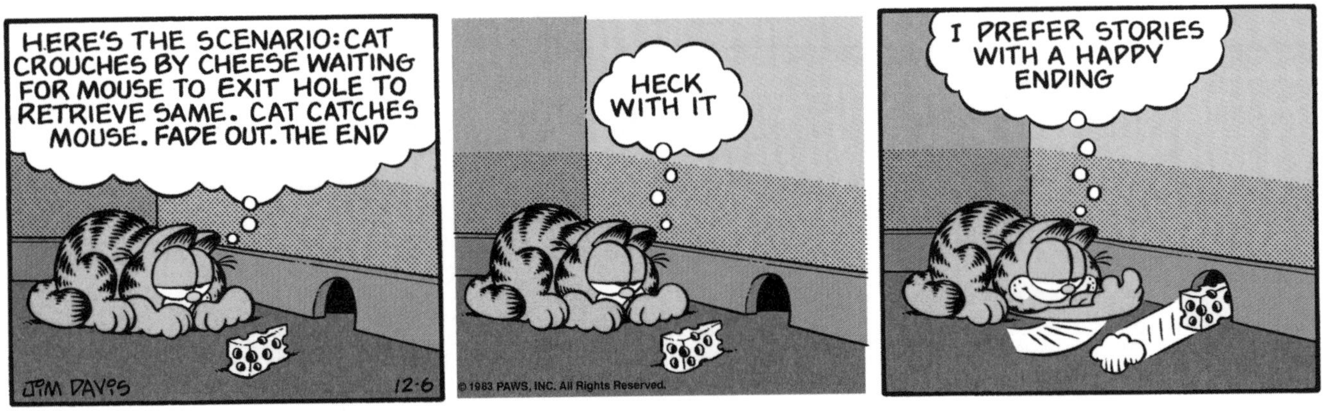
HERE'S THE SCENARIO: CAT CROUCHES BY CHEESE WAITING FOR MOUSE TO EXIT HOLE TO RETRIEVE SAME. CAT CATCHES MOUSE. FADE OUT. THE END
HECK WITH IT
I PREFER STORIES WITH A HAPPY ENDING
JIM DAVIS 12·6
© 1983 PAWS, INC. All Rights Reserved.

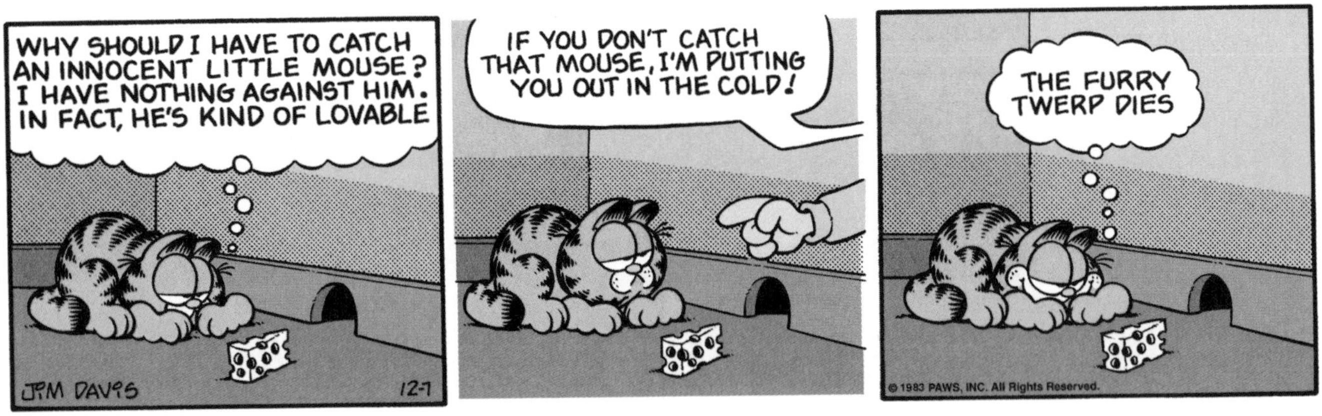
WHY SHOULD I HAVE TO CATCH AN INNOCENT LITTLE MOUSE? I HAVE NOTHING AGAINST HIM. IN FACT, HE'S KIND OF LOVABLE
IF YOU DON'T CATCH THAT MOUSE, I'M PUTTING YOU OUT IN THE COLD!
THE FURRY TWERP DIES
JIM DAVIS 12-7
© 1983 PAWS, INC. All Rights Reserved.

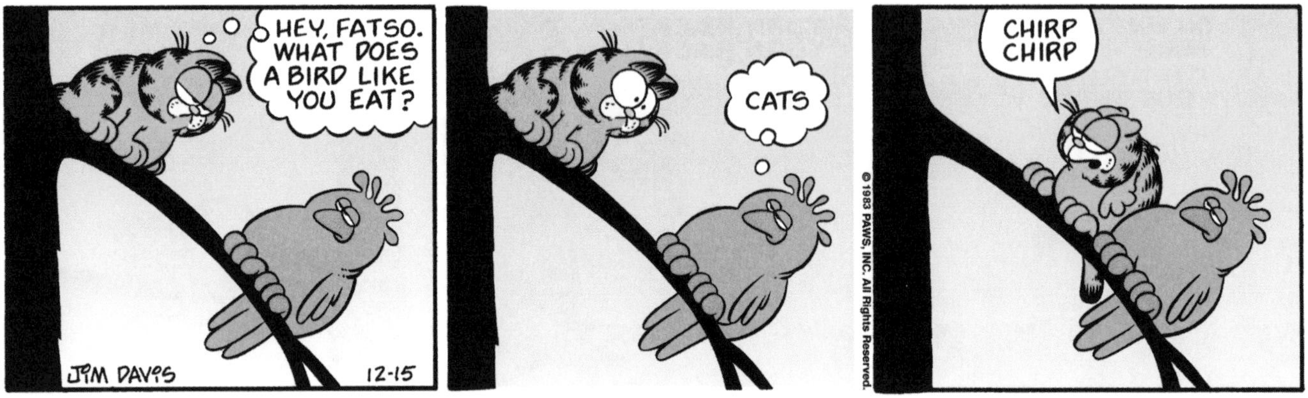
HEY, FATSO. WHAT DOES A BIRD LIKE YOU EAT?
JIM DAVIS
12-15
CATS
© 1983 PAWS, INC. All Rights Reserved.
CHIRP CHIRP

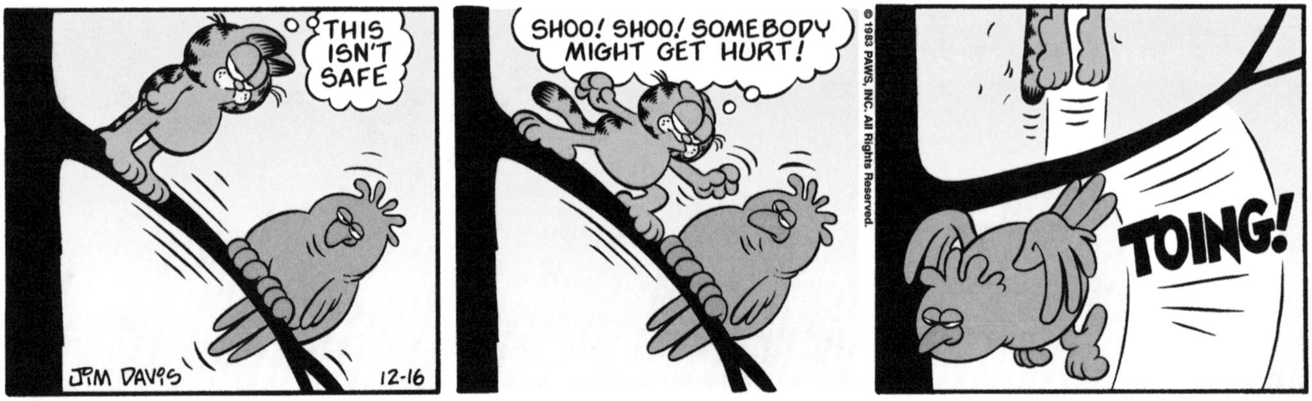
THIS ISN'T SAFE
JIM DAVIS
12-16
SHOO! SHOO! SOMEBODY MIGHT GET HURT!
© 1983 PAWS, INC. All Rights Reserved.
TOING!

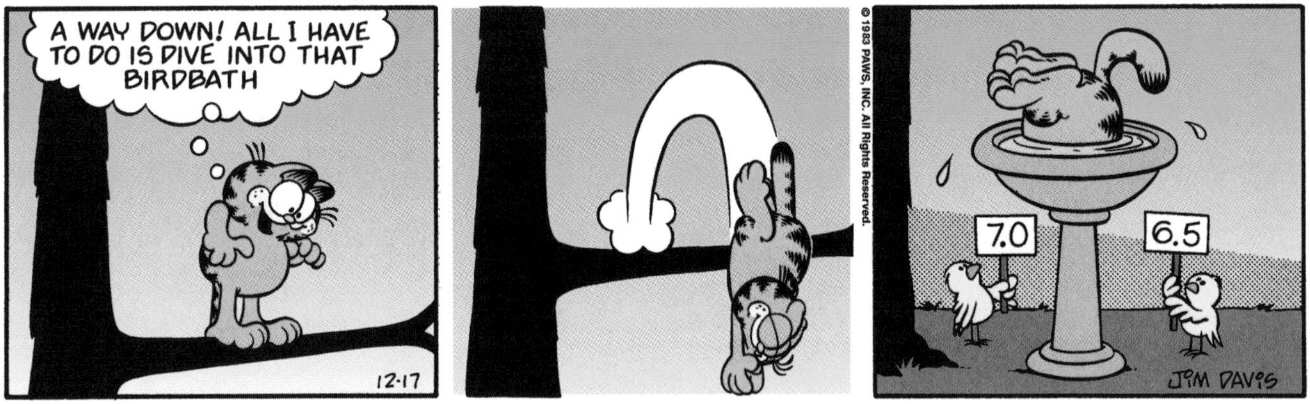
A WAY DOWN! ALL I HAVE TO DO IS DIVE INTO THAT BIRDBATH
12-17
© 1983 PAWS, INC. All Rights Reserved.
7.0
6.5
JIM DAVIS

'Twas the night before Christmas, when all through the house Not a creature was stirring, not even a mouse; The stockings were hung by the chimney with care, In hopes that St. Nicholas soon would be there;

FILL THIS ONE, SANTA!

The children were nestled all snug in their beds, While visions of sugarplums danced in their heads;

NOW GIMME A VISION OF LASAGNA

And Mamma in her 'kerchief, and I in my cap, Had just settled our brains for a long winter's nap,

THIS IS MY KIND OF STORY

When out on the lawn there arose such a clatter, I sprang from the bed to see what was the matter. Away to the window I flew like a flash, Tore open the shutters and threw up the sash.

WHAT'S A SASH?

The moon on the breast of the new-fallen snow Gave the luster of midday to objects below, When, what to my wondering eyes should appear, But a miniature sleigh, and eight tiny reindeer,

THEY LOOK BIGGER ON TELEVISION

With a little old driver, so lively and quick, I knew in a moment it must be St. Nick.

OR MAYBE SANTA CLAUS

More rapid than eagles his coursers they came, And he whistled, and shouted, and called them by name; "Now, Dasher! Now, Dancer! Now, Prancer and Vixen! On, Comet! On, Cupid! On, Donder and Blitzen!

ON, DOPEY! ON, SNEEZY! ON, HAPPY!

"To the top of the porch! To the top of the wall! Now dash away! Dash away! Dash away all!"

CAN'T THEY JUST WALK ANYWHERE?

As dry leaves that before the wild hurricane fly, When they meet with an obstacle, mount to the sky, So up to the housetop the coursers they flew, With the sleigh full of toys, and St. Nicholas, too.

TUNE IN TOMORROW. THE GOOD PART'S COMING

JIM DAVIS 12-19

JIM DAVIS 12-20

JIM DAVIS 12-21

And then, in a twinkling, I heard on the roof
The prancing and pawing of each little hoof.
As I drew in my head, and was turning around,
Down the chimney St. Nicholas came with a bound.

OH, NO! A CHIMNEY MONSTER!

He was dressed all in fur, from his head to his foot,
And his clothes were all tarnished with ashes and soot;
A bundle of toys he had flung on his back,
And he looked like a peddler just opening his pack.

YOU DIDN'T BREAK ANY TOYS, DID YOU?

His eyes — how they twinkled! His dimples how merry!
His cheeks were like roses, his nose like a cherry!
His droll little mouth was drawn up like a bow,
And the beard on his chin was as white as the snow;

HE ALSO HAS A WELL-ROUNDED PERSONALITY

The stump of a pipe he held tight in his teeth,
And the smoke it encircled his head like a wreath;
He had a broad face and a little round belly
That shook when he laughed, like a bowlful of jelly.

HO! HO! HO!

A FEW SIT-UPS WOULD TAKE CARE OF THAT, FELLA

He was chubby and plump, a right jolly old elf,
And I laughed when I saw him, in spite of myself;
A wink of his eye and a twist of his head
Soon gave me to know I had nothing to dread.

WE MUST HAVE LUNCH SOMETIME

He spoke not a word, but went straight to his work,
And filled all the stockings; then turned with a jerk,
And laying his finger aside of his nose,
And giving a nod, up the chimney he rose;

HOW DID HE DO THAT?

He sprang to his sleigh, to his team gave a whistle,
And away they all flew like the down of a thistle.
But I heard him exclaim, ere he drove out of sight,

HAPPY CHRISTMAS TO ALL AND TO ALL A GOOD NIGHT!

WHAT A NICE GUY. WHAT A NICE STORY

HAVE A HAPPY AND LOVING HOLIDAY SEASON

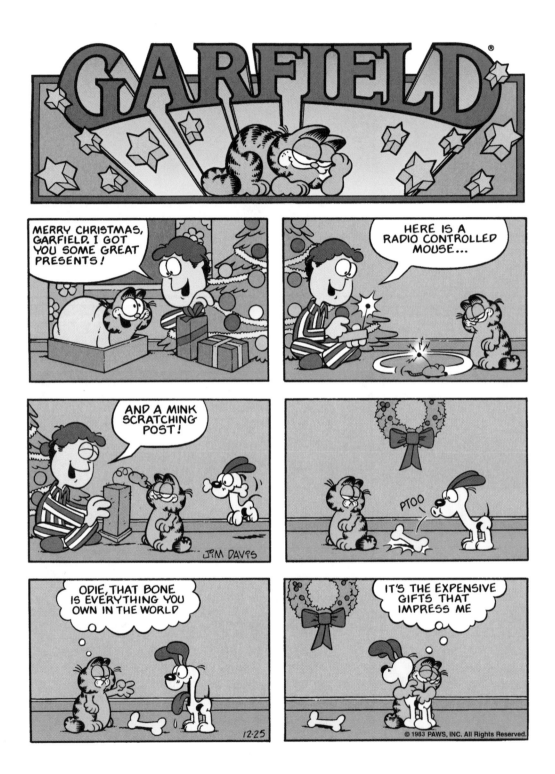

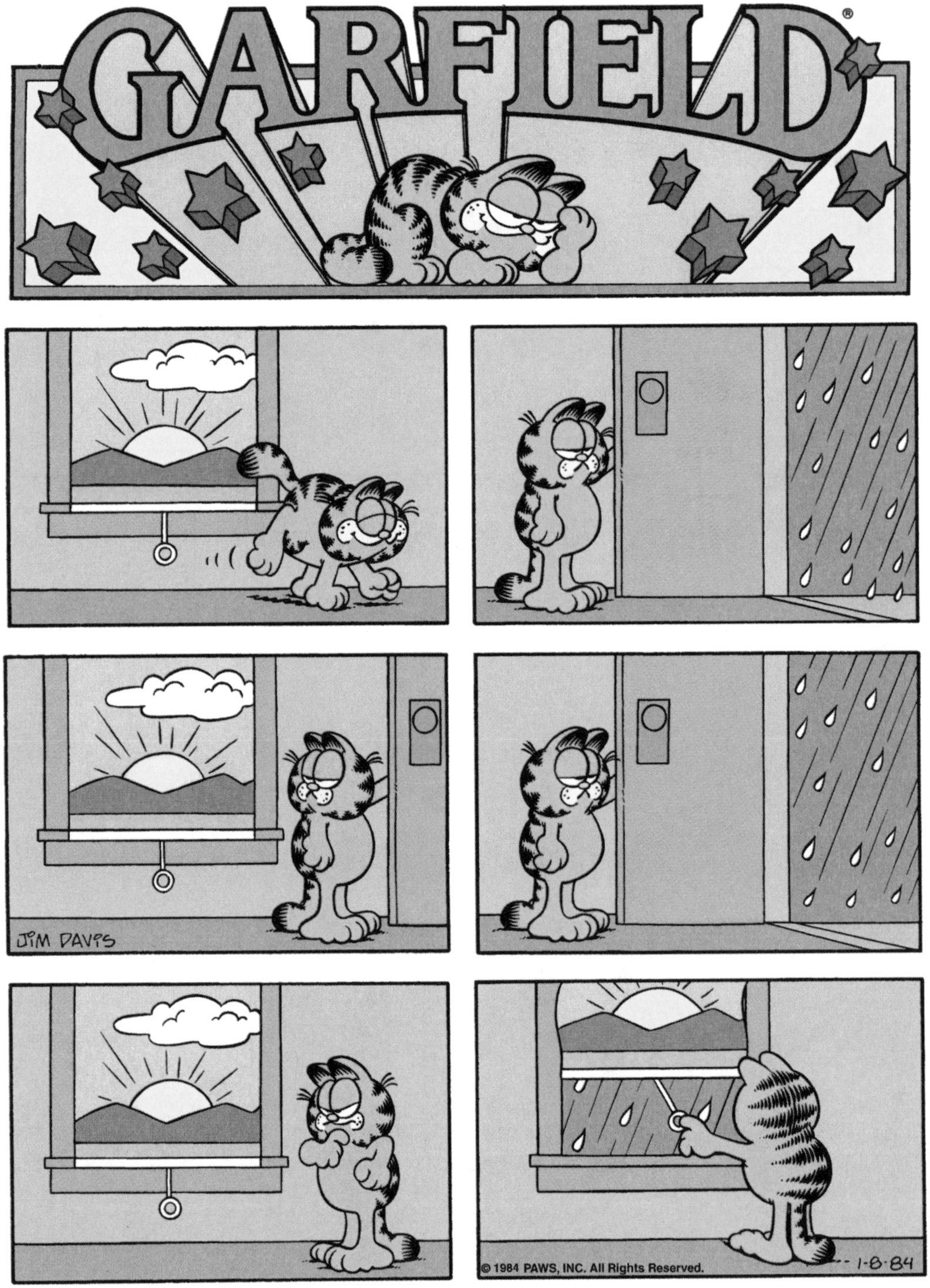
GARFIELD®
JIM DAVIS
© 1984 PAWS, INC. All Rights Reserved.
1-8-84

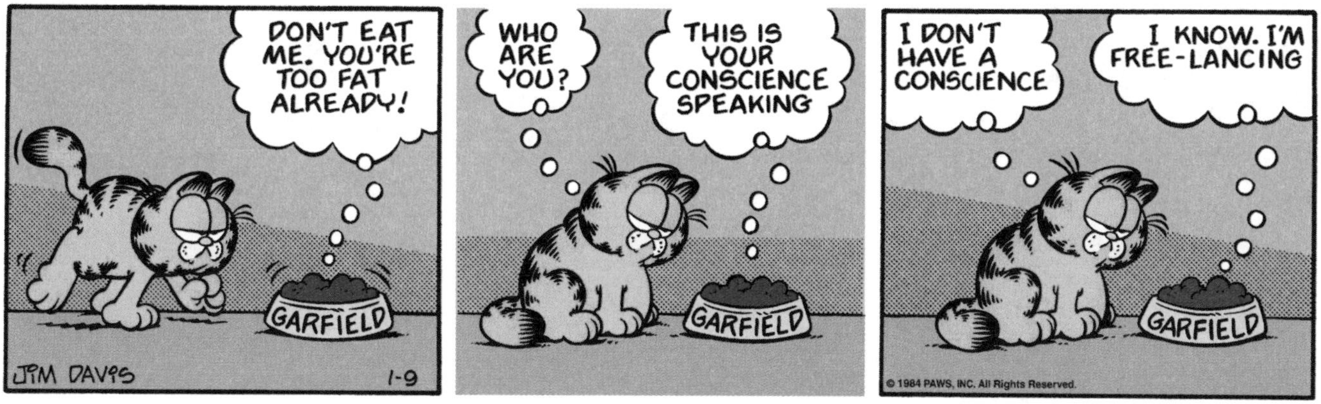
DON'T EAT ME. YOU'RE TOO FAT ALREADY!
GARFIELD
JIM DAVIS
1-9
WHO ARE YOU?
THIS IS YOUR CONSCIENCE SPEAKING
GARFIELD
I DON'T HAVE A CONSCIENCE
I KNOW. I'M FREE-LANCING
GARFIELD
© 1984 PAWS, INC. All Rights Reserved.

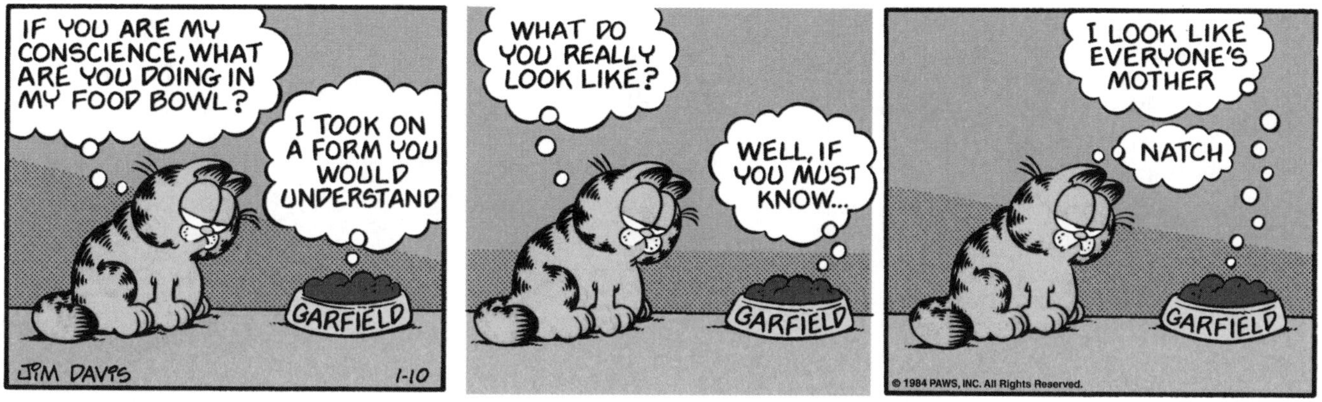
IF YOU ARE MY CONSCIENCE, WHAT ARE YOU DOING IN MY FOOD BOWL?
I TOOK ON A FORM YOU WOULD UNDERSTAND
GARFIELD
JIM DAVIS
1-10
WHAT DO YOU REALLY LOOK LIKE?
WELL, IF YOU MUST KNOW...
GARFIELD
I LOOK LIKE EVERYONE'S MOTHER
NATCH
GARFIELD
© 1984 PAWS, INC. All Rights Reserved.

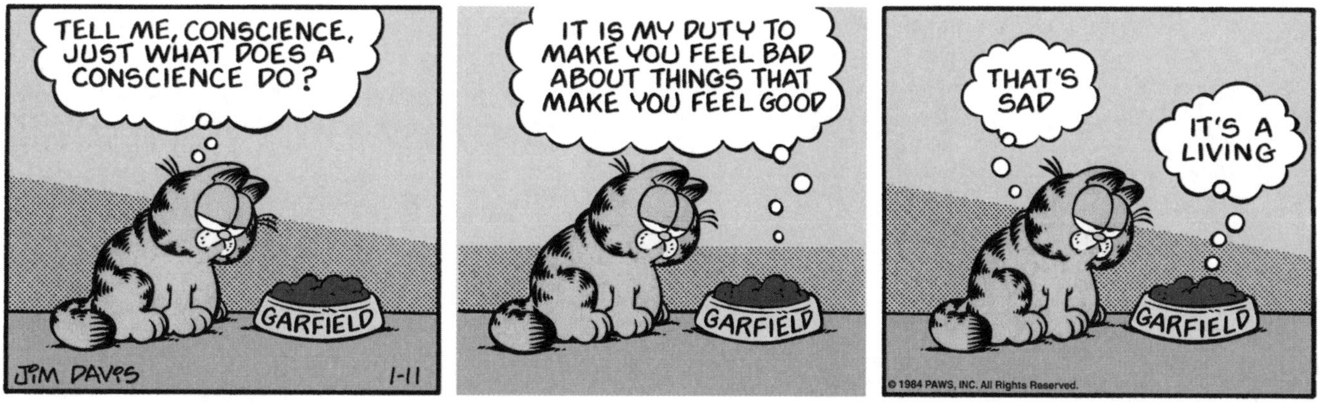
TELL ME, CONSCIENCE, JUST WHAT DOES A CONSCIENCE DO?
GARFIELD
JIM DAVIS
1-11
IT IS MY DUTY TO MAKE YOU FEEL BAD ABOUT THINGS THAT MAKE YOU FEEL GOOD
GARFIELD
THAT'S SAD
IT'S A LIVING
GARFIELD
© 1984 PAWS, INC. All Rights Reserved.

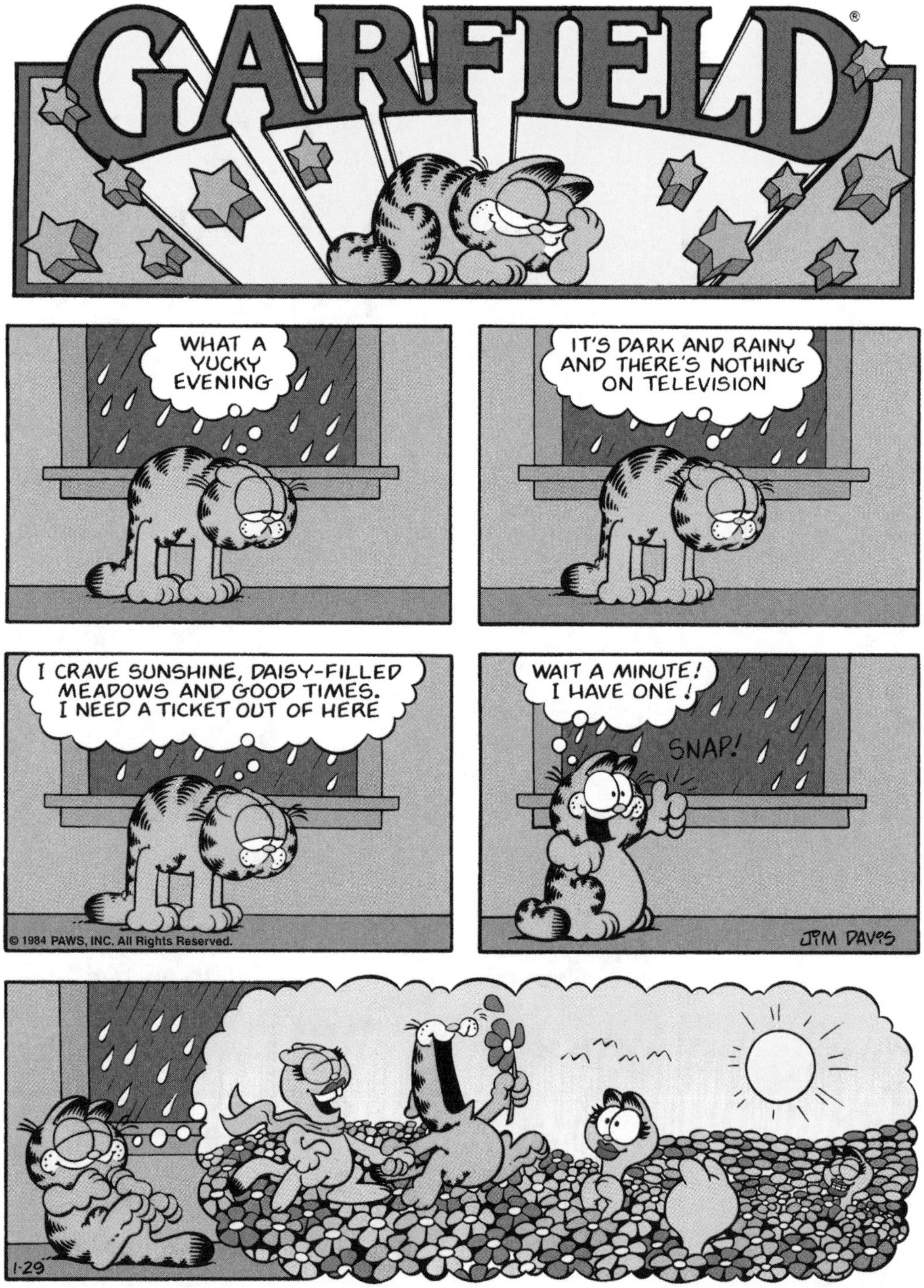
GARFIELD®
WHAT A YUCKY EVENING
IT'S DARK AND RAINY AND THERE'S NOTHING ON TELEVISION
I CRAVE SUNSHINE, DAISY-FILLED MEADOWS AND GOOD TIMES. I NEED A TICKET OUT OF HERE
WAIT A MINUTE! I HAVE ONE!
SNAP!
© 1984 PAWS, INC. All Rights Reserved.
JIM DAVIS
1-29

47

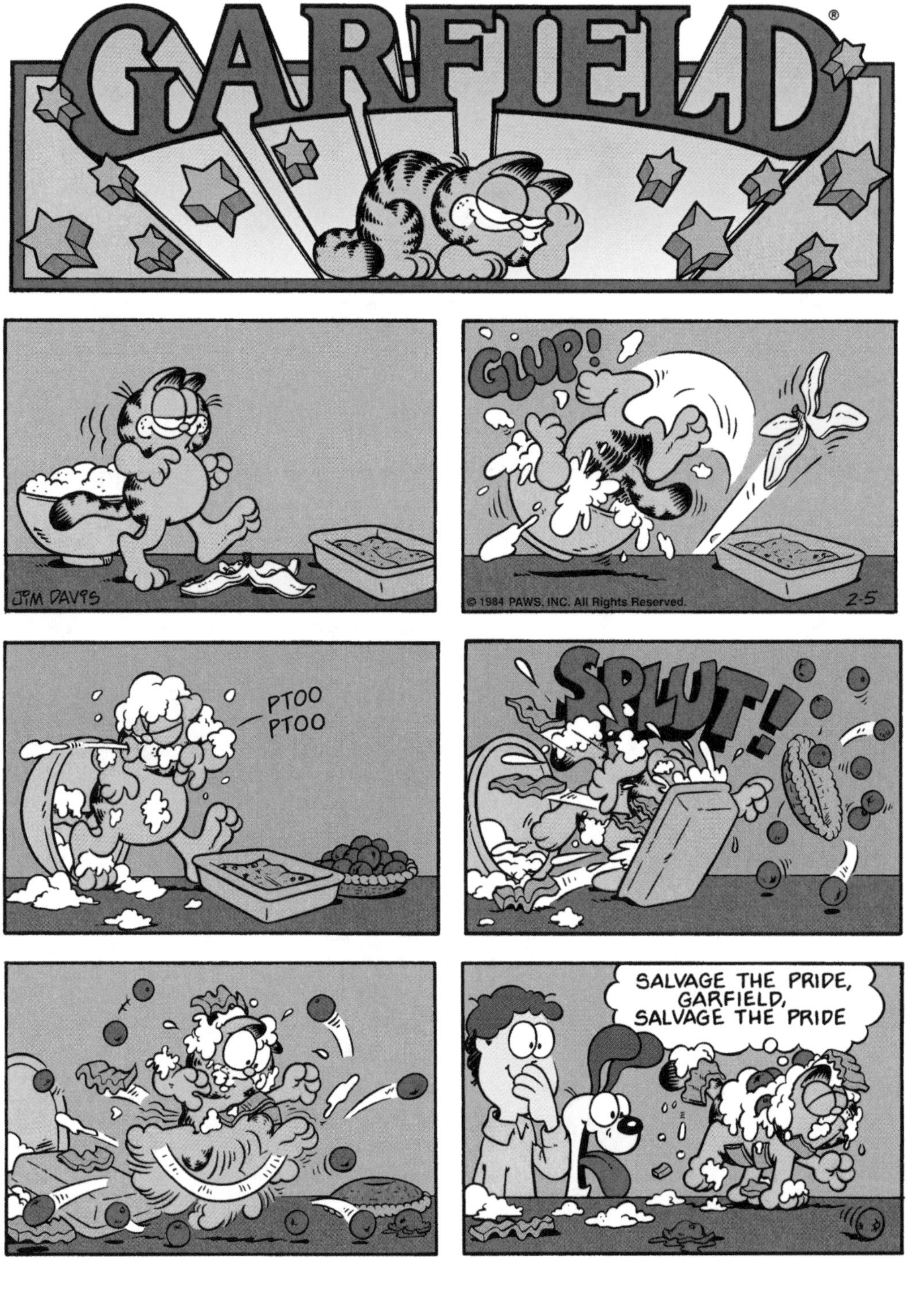
GARFIELD
JIM DAVIS
GLUP!
© 1984 PAWS, INC. All Rights Reserved.
2-5
PTOO PTOO
SPLUT!
SALVAGE THE PRIDE, GARFIELD, SALVAGE THE PRIDE

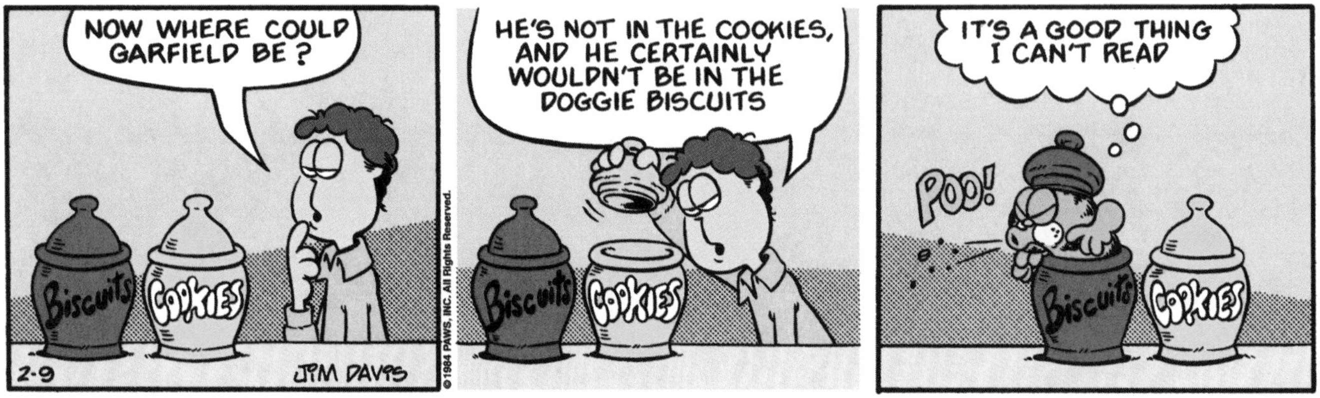
NOW WHERE COULD GARFIELD BE ?
Biscuits
COOKIES
2-9
JIM DAVIS
© 1984 PAWS, INC. All Rights Reserved.
HE'S NOT IN THE COOKIES, AND HE CERTAINLY WOULDN'T BE IN THE DOGGIE BISCUITS
Biscuits
COOKIES
IT'S A GOOD THING I CAN'T READ
POO!
Biscuits
COOKIES

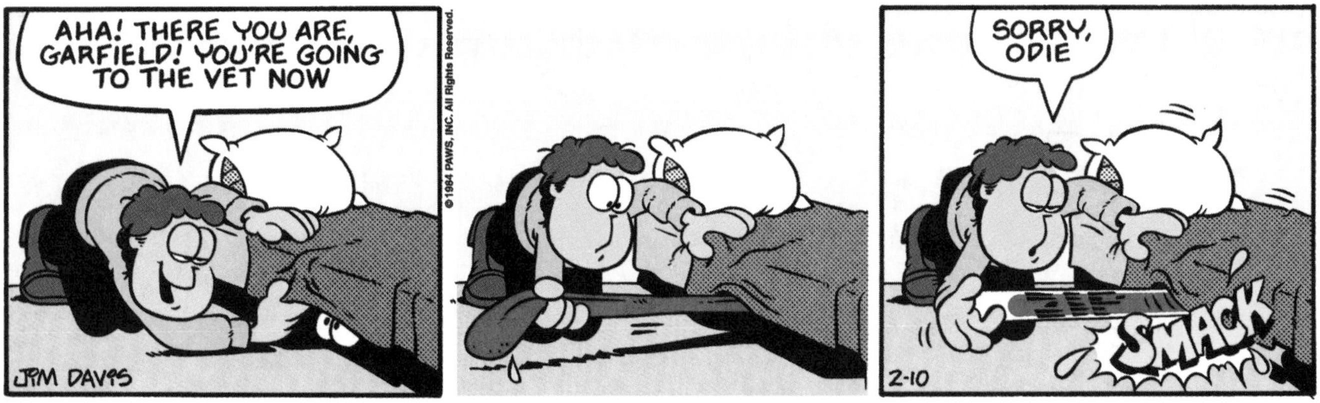
AHA! THERE YOU ARE, GARFIELD! YOU'RE GOING TO THE VET NOW
JIM DAVIS
© 1984 PAWS, INC. All Rights Reserved.
SORRY, ODIE
SMACK
2-10

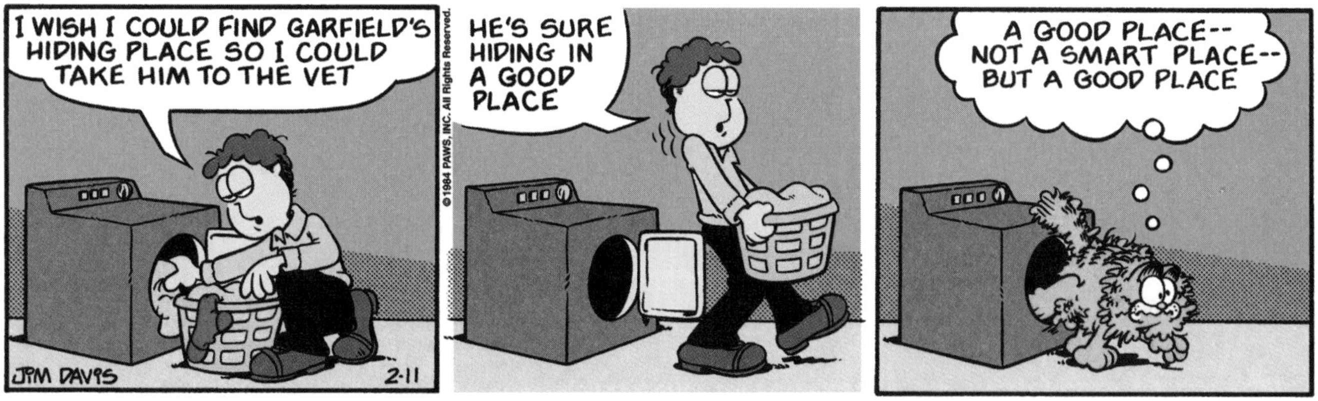
I WISH I COULD FIND GARFIELD'S HIDING PLACE SO I COULD TAKE HIM TO THE VET
JIM DAVIS
2-11
© 1984 PAWS, INC. All Rights Reserved.
HE'S SURE HIDING IN A GOOD PLACE
A GOOD PLACE-- NOT A SMART PLACE-- BUT A GOOD PLACE

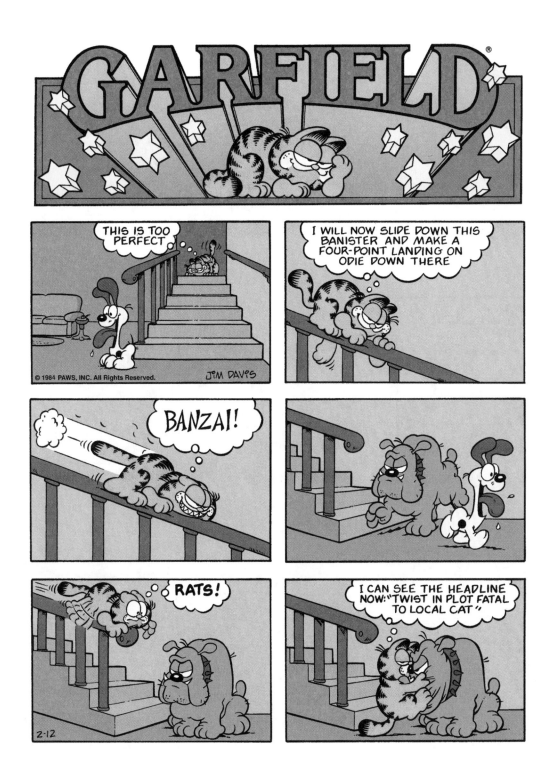

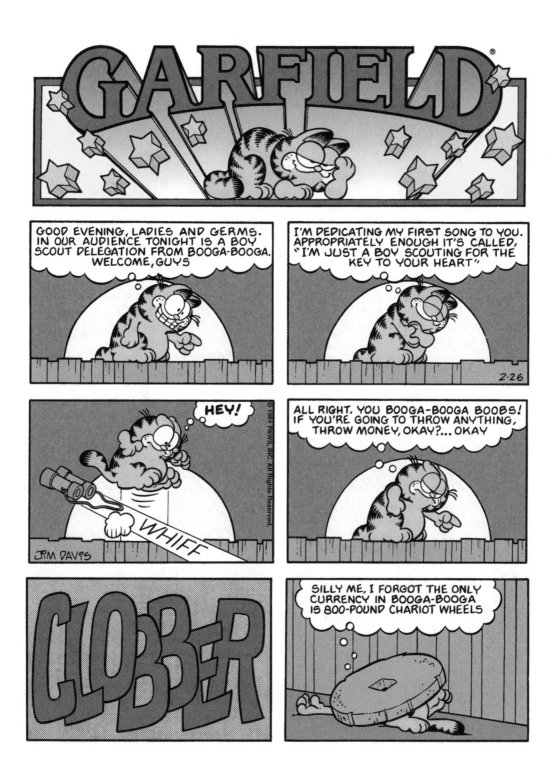

57

61

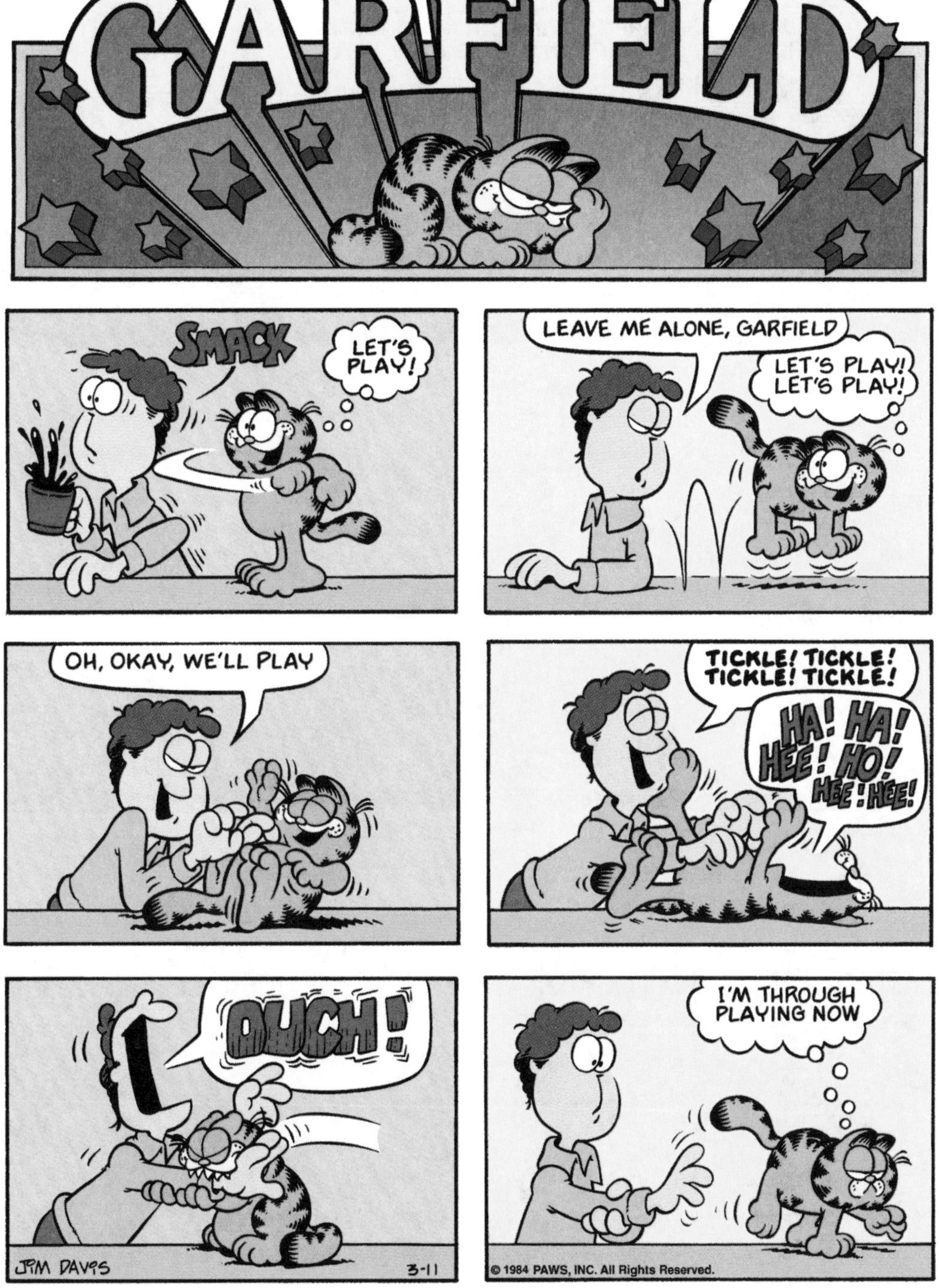
GARFIELD®
SMACK
LET'S PLAY!
LEAVE ME ALONE, GARFIELD
LET'S PLAY! LET'S PLAY!
OH, OKAY, WE'LL PLAY
TICKLE! TICKLE! TICKLE! TICKLE!
HA! HA! HEE! HO! HEE! HEE!
OUCH!
I'M THROUGH PLAYING NOW
JIM DAVIS
3-11
© 1984 PAWS, INC. All Rights Reserved.

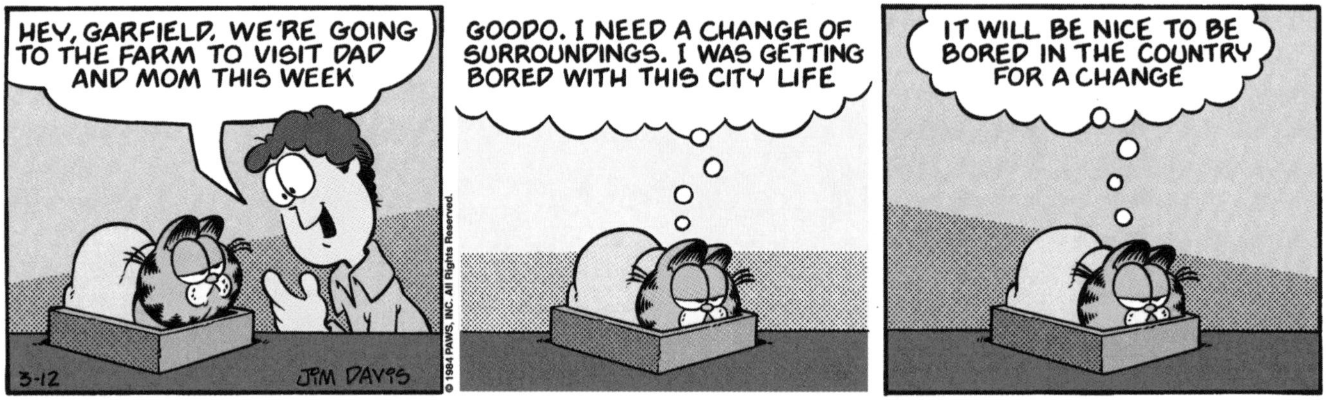
HEY, GARFIELD. WE'RE GOING TO THE FARM TO VISIT DAD AND MOM THIS WEEK
3-12
JIM DAVIS
© 1984 PAWS, INC. All Rights Reserved.
GOODO. I NEED A CHANGE OF SURROUNDINGS. I WAS GETTING BORED WITH THIS CITY LIFE
IT WILL BE NICE TO BE BORED IN THE COUNTRY FOR A CHANGE

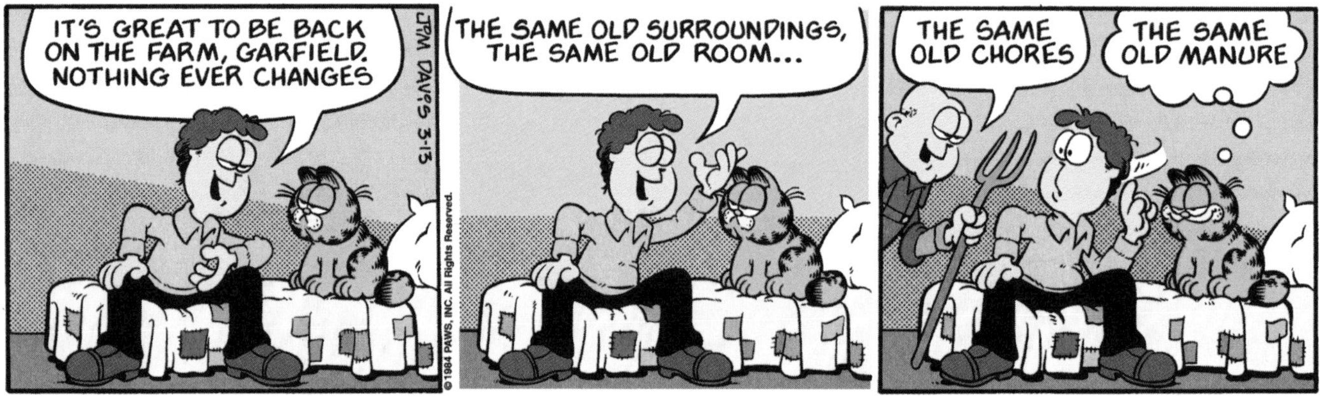
IT'S GREAT TO BE BACK ON THE FARM, GARFIELD. NOTHING EVER CHANGES
JIM DAVIS 3-13
© 1984 PAWS, INC. All Rights Reserved.
THE SAME OLD SURROUNDINGS, THE SAME OLD ROOM...
THE SAME OLD CHORES
THE SAME OLD MANURE

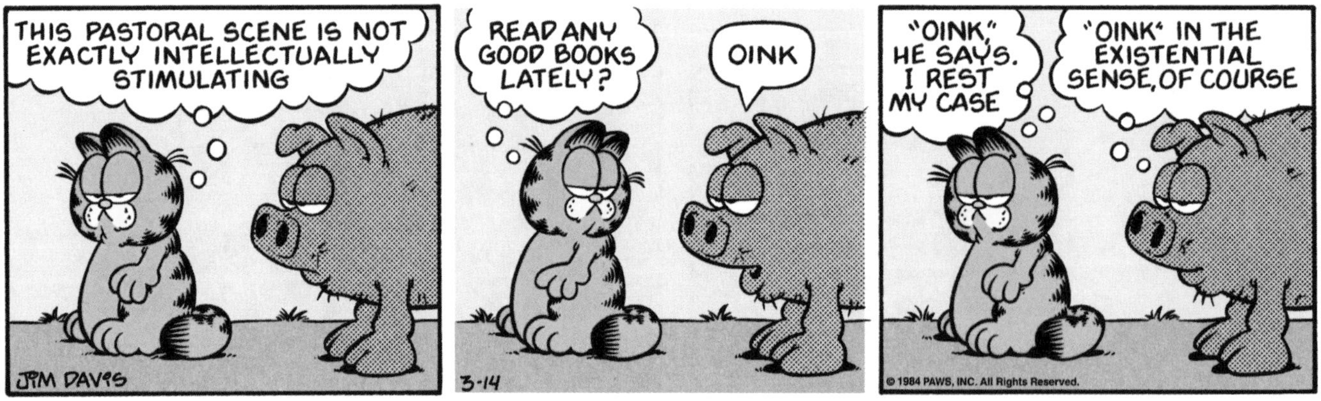
THIS PASTORAL SCENE IS NOT EXACTLY INTELLECTUALLY STIMULATING
JIM DAVIS
READ ANY GOOD BOOKS LATELY?
OINK
3-14
"OINK," HE SAYS. I REST MY CASE
"OINK" IN THE EXISTENTIAL SENSE, OF COURSE
© 1984 PAWS, INC. All Rights Reserved.

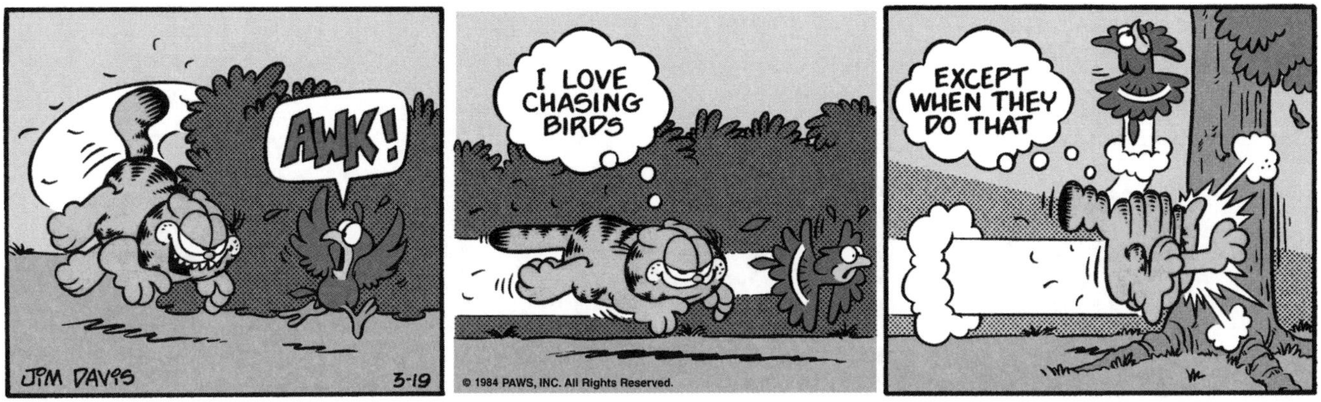
AWK!
JIM DAVIS
3-19
I LOVE CHASING BIRDS
© 1984 PAWS, INC. All Rights Reserved.
EXCEPT WHEN THEY DO THAT

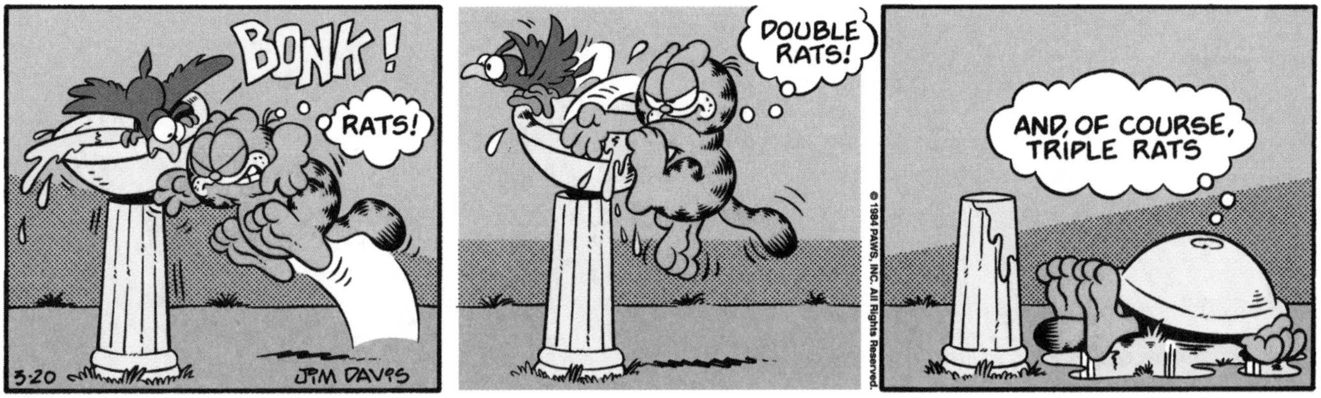
BONK!
RATS!
3-20
JIM DAVIS
DOUBLE RATS!
© 1984 PAWS, INC. All Rights Reserved.
AND, OF COURSE, TRIPLE RATS

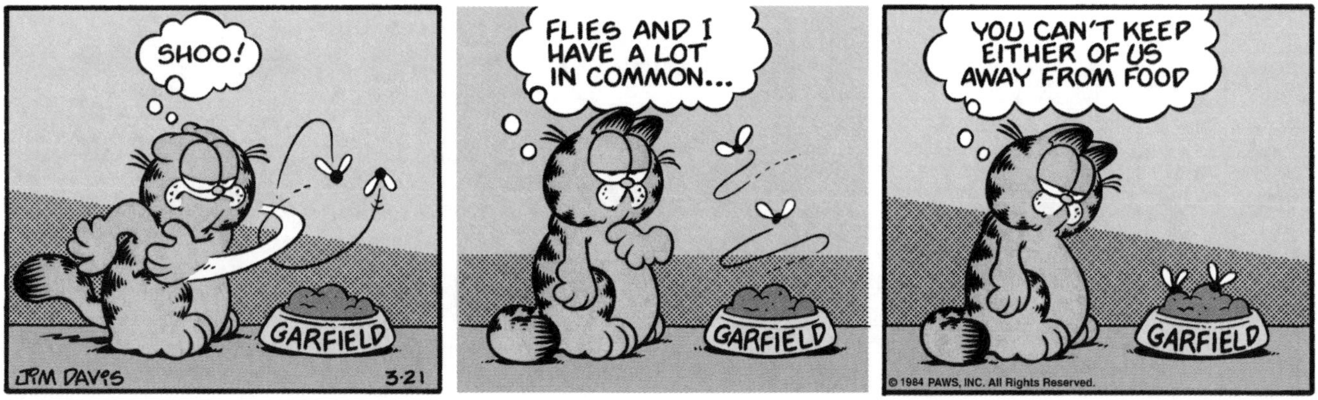
SHOO!
GARFIELD
JIM DAVIS
3-21
FLIES AND I HAVE A LOT IN COMMON...
GARFIELD
YOU CAN'T KEEP EITHER OF US AWAY FROM FOOD
GARFIELD
© 1984 PAWS, INC. All Rights Reserved.

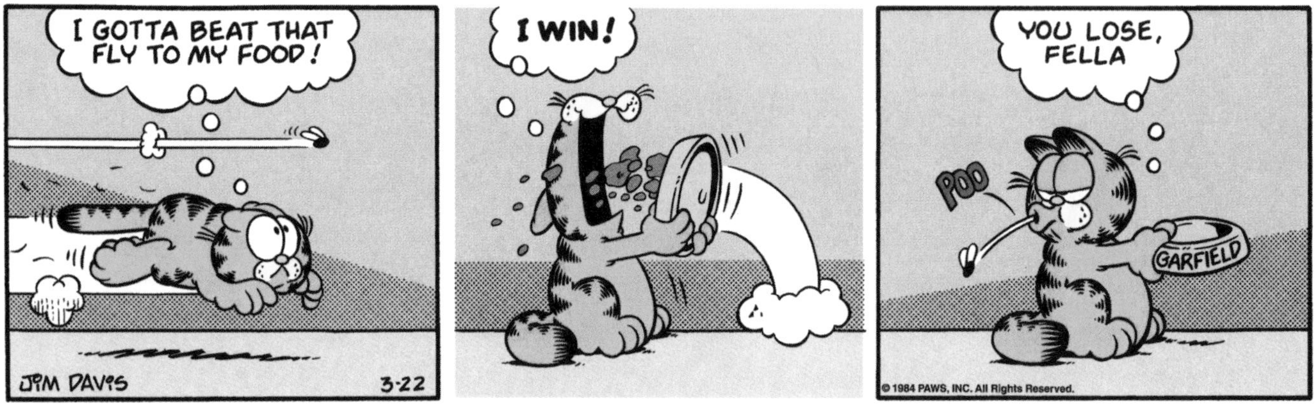
I GOTTA BEAT THAT FLY TO MY FOOD!
JIM DAVIS
3-22
I WIN!
YOU LOSE, FELLA
POO
GARFIELD
© 1984 PAWS, INC. All Rights Reserved.

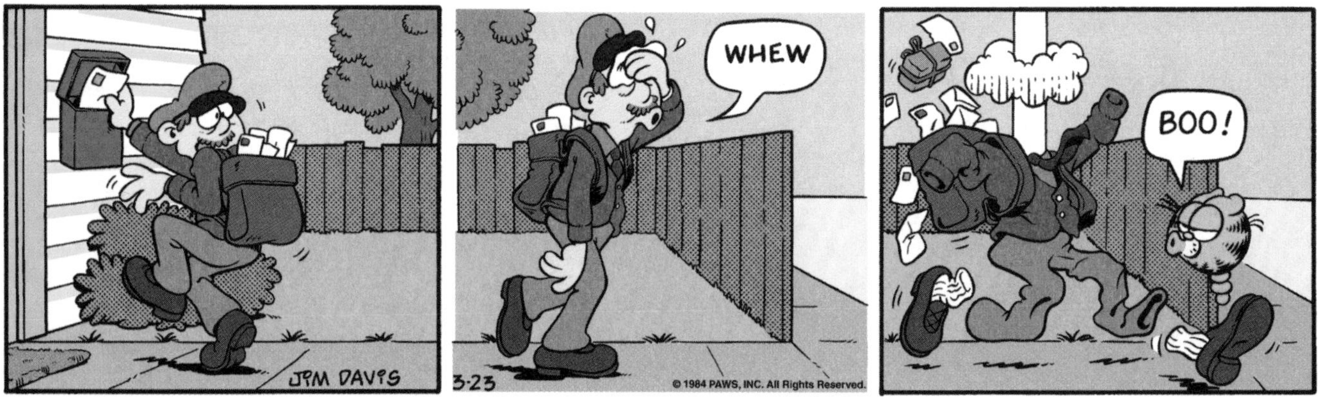
JIM DAVIS
WHEW
3-23
© 1984 PAWS, INC. All Rights Reserved.
BOO!

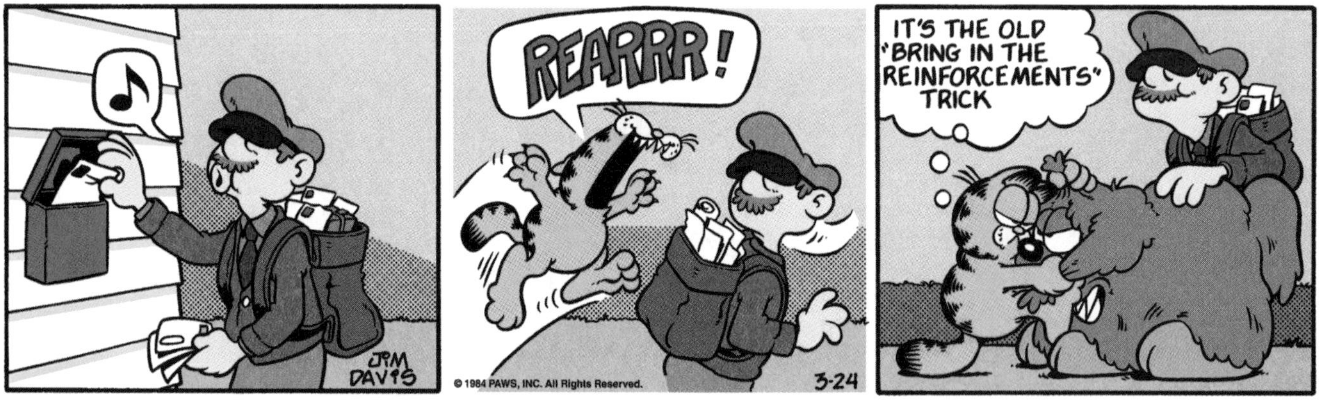
JIM DAVIS
REARRR!
© 1984 PAWS, INC. All Rights Reserved.
3-24
IT'S THE OLD "BRING IN THE REINFORCEMENTS" TRICK

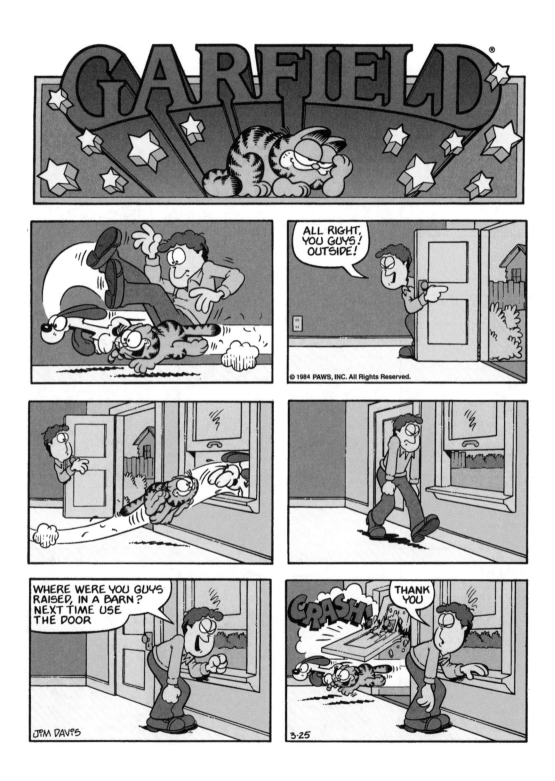

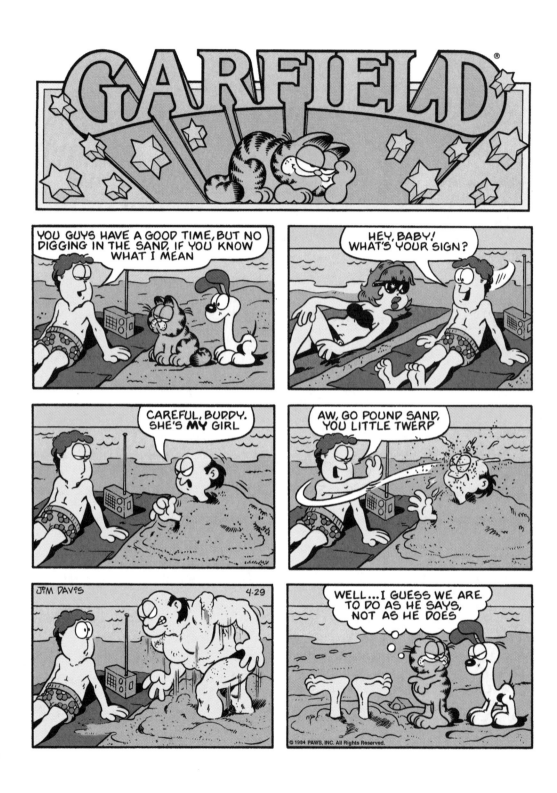

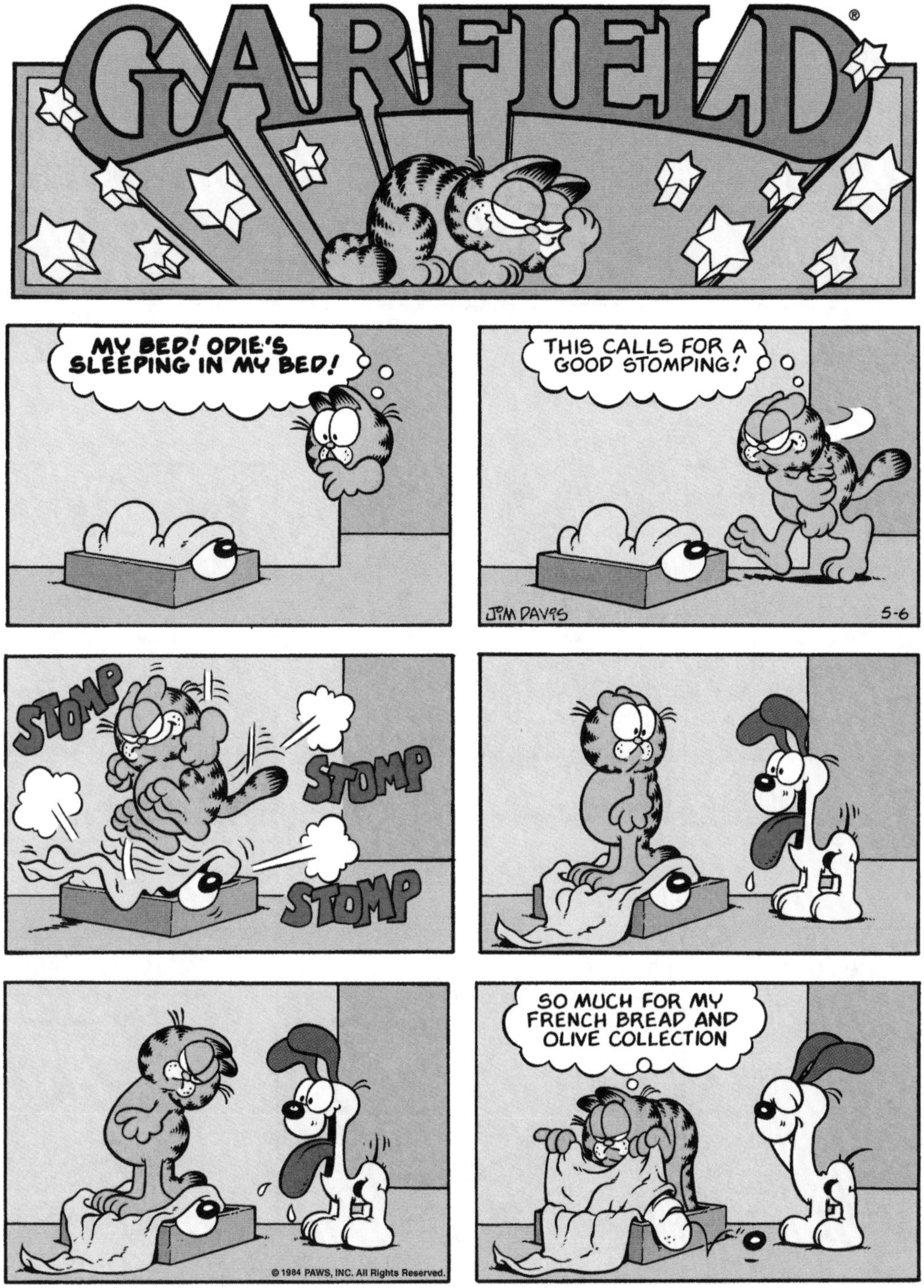
GARFIELD®
MY BED! ODIE'S SLEEPING IN MY BED!
THIS CALLS FOR A GOOD STOMPING!
JIM DAVIS
5-6
STOMP
STOMP
STOMP
© 1984 PAWS, INC. All Rights Reserved.
SO MUCH FOR MY FRENCH BREAD AND OLIVE COLLECTION

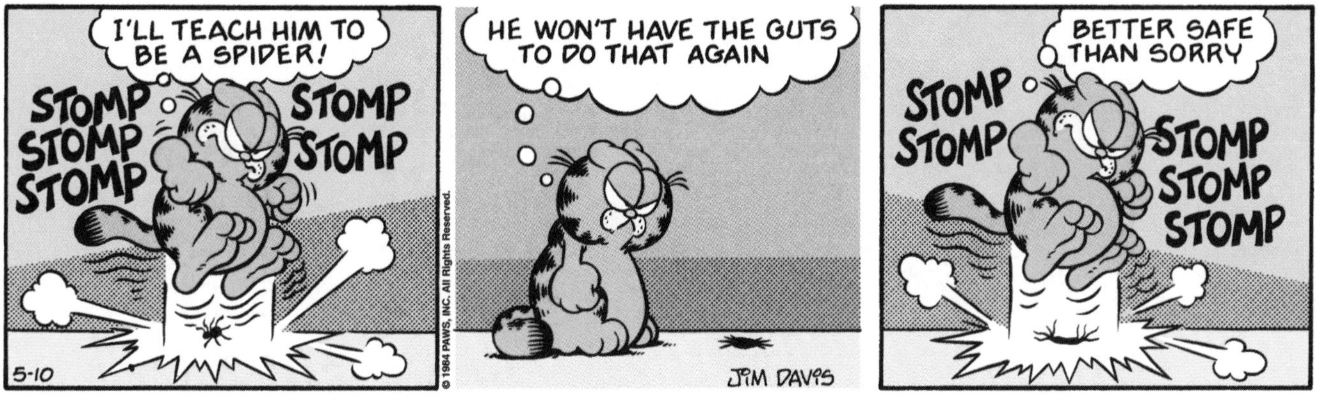
I'LL TEACH HIM TO BE A SPIDER!
STOMP STOMP STOMP
STOMP STOMP
5-10
© 1984 PAWS, INC. All Rights Reserved.
HE WON'T HAVE THE GUTS TO DO THAT AGAIN
JIM DAVIS
BETTER SAFE THAN SORRY
STOMP STOMP
STOMP STOMP STOMP

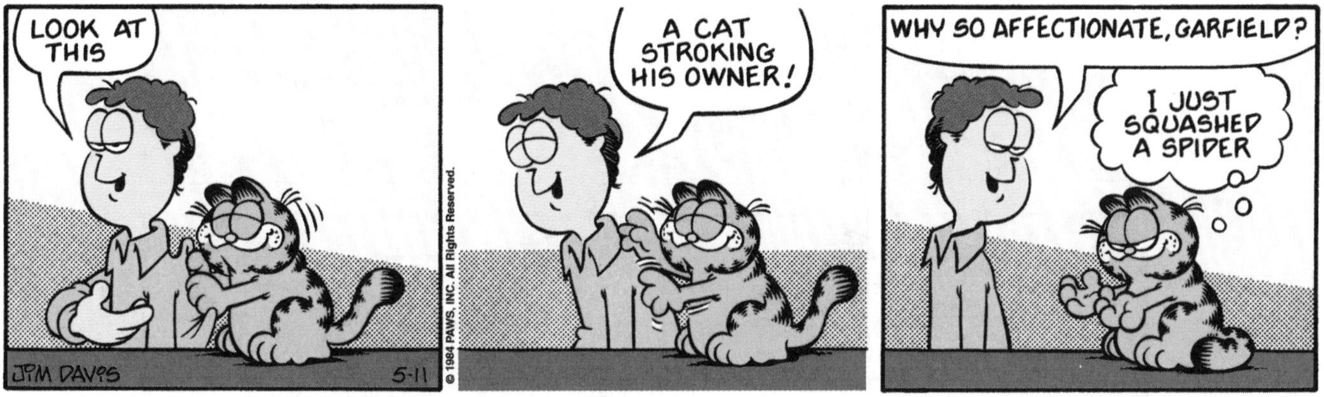
LOOK AT THIS
JIM DAVIS
5-11
© 1984 PAWS, INC. All Rights Reserved.
A CAT STROKING HIS OWNER!
WHY SO AFFECTIONATE, GARFIELD?
I JUST SQUASHED A SPIDER

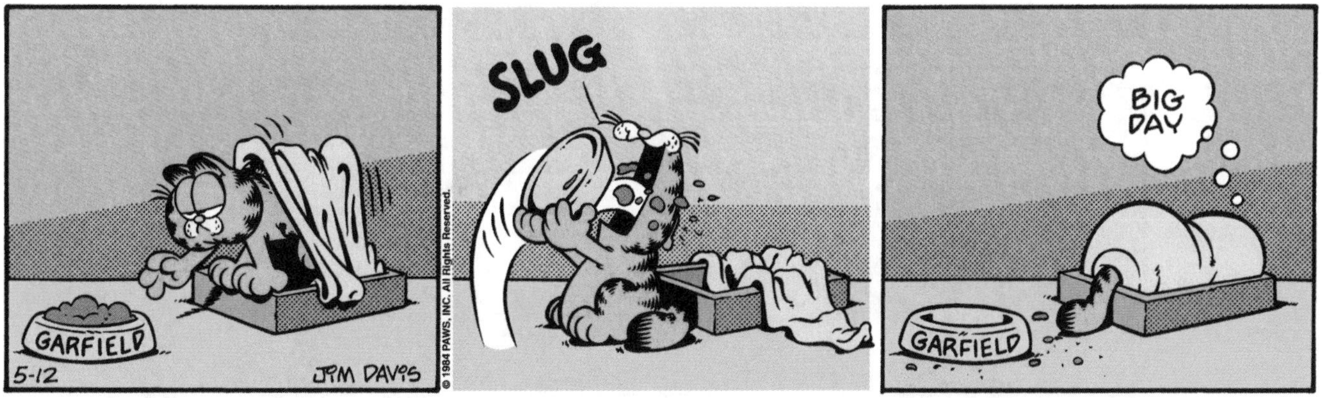
GARFIELD
5-12
JIM DAVIS
© 1984 PAWS, INC. All Rights Reserved.
SLUG
BIG DAY
GARFIELD

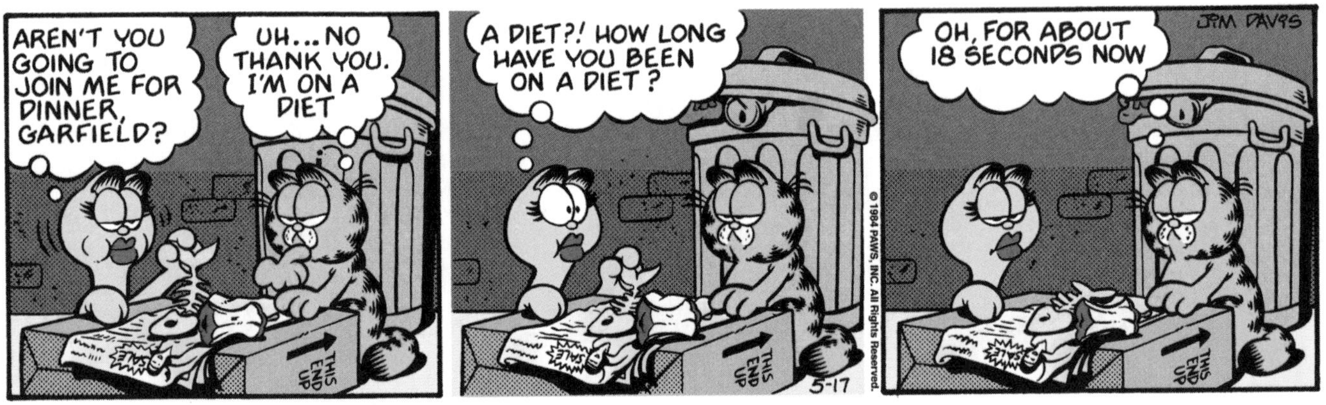
ARE'N'T YOU GOING TO JOIN ME FOR DINNER, GARFIELD?
UH... NO THANK YOU. I'M ON A DIET
A DIET?! HOW LONG HAVE YOU BEEN ON A DIET?
OH, FOR ABOUT 18 SECONDS NOW
JIM DAVIS
5-17
© 1984 PAWS, INC. All Rights Reserved.
THIS END UP
SALE

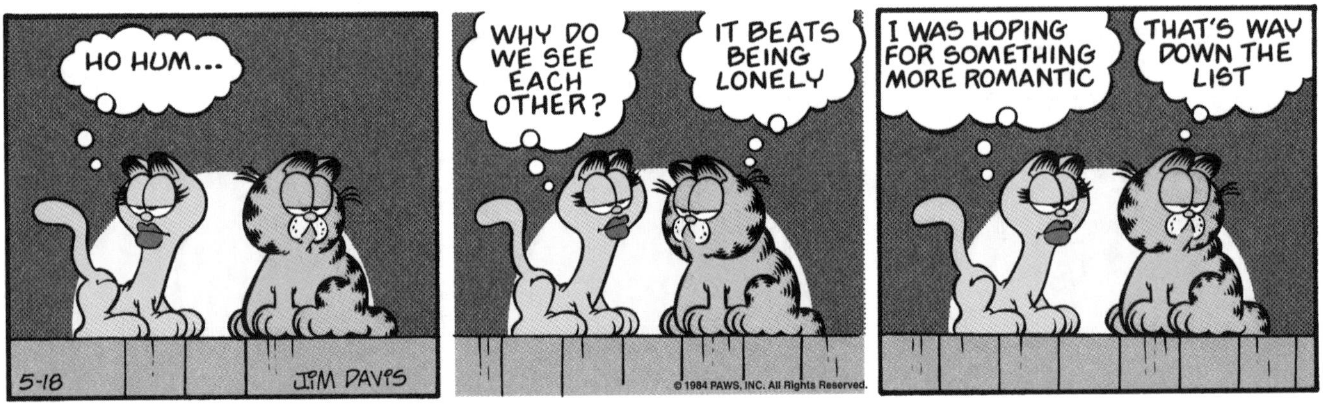
HO HUM...
5-18
JIM DAVIS
WHY DO WE SEE EACH OTHER?
IT BEATS BEING LONELY
© 1984 PAWS, INC. All Rights Reserved.
I WAS HOPING FOR SOMETHING MORE ROMANTIC
THAT'S WAY DOWN THE LIST

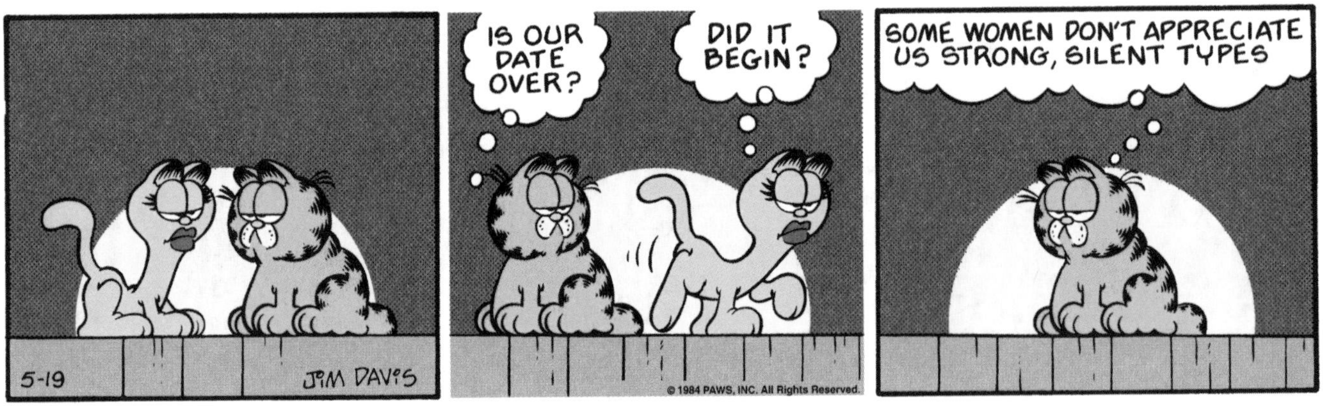
5-19
JIM DAVIS
IS OUR DATE OVER?
DID IT BEGIN?
© 1984 PAWS, INC. All Rights Reserved.
SOME WOMEN DON'T APPRECIATE US STRONG, SILENT TYPES

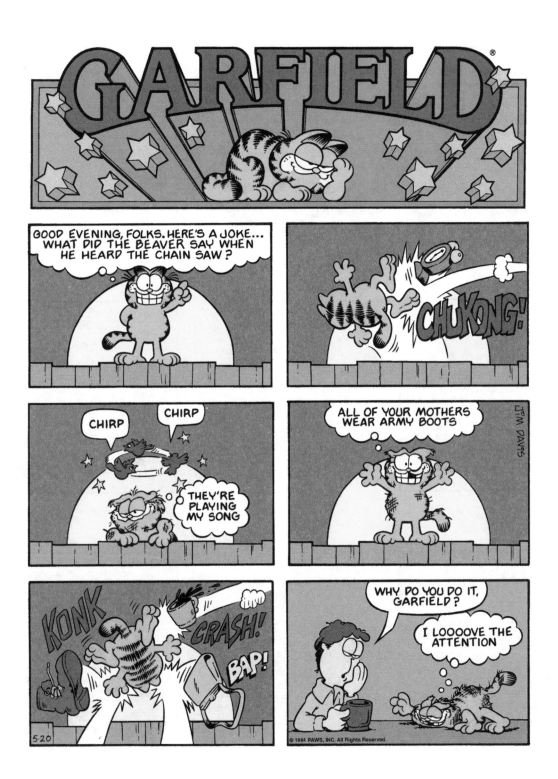